Emma

—for Ann Smith, in memoriam

Emma

SJ

copyright © 2025 by Russell Helms

Please contact the publisher for permission to reprint content from this novel.

ISBN: 978-1-943661-61-9

Sij Books
booksbysij@gmail.com

Printed in the USA

MULDRAUGH, KENTUCKY

A year later, after I married Reece, protests fizzled, but tension between the followers of Julia, Dahlia, and the traditional Gods continue. The Southern Baptist Convention of churches has been gutted, with nearly eighty percent of churches claiming independence under the good gaze of Julia. Followers of Dahlia, although a minority, cling to their belief that evil is necessary for good, like yeast leavening bread. Reece and I moved from Fort Knox to the nearby town of Muldraugh. Dr. Markush fought us, fearing for our safety still, but he ultimately relented.

Our two-story home dates from the 1930s, white and square, set back on a long, narrow lot. There are four large bedrooms and an ample attic space with four dormers. Organon footed the purchase, and we receive a monthly stipend to pay the bills. Due to our chromosomal differences, a child is not possible, but we try hard nonetheless. Pundits are gaga at what might be produced.

Outside, a chilly March breeze rustles the trees at the front of the yard as Reece washes dishes in the kitchen. The large kitchen, dated from the 1960s, features yellow laminate countertops and an old-fashioned fridge with a latching metal handle. I sit at the kitchen farm table, coddling a cup of fresh coffee, gazing at him. A tight t-shirt hugs his slim body.

"What do we work on today?" A major publisher is shepherding us through a book project about our wild adventure with Dahlia.

Reece rinses suds from a glass. "We left off with us

meeting in Gwar. The little army of Dahlia lookalikes had burst through the gate with knives. I found Mia. Then, *poof,* we were transported to my backyard in Richmond. I've never been so confused as I was that day."

I laugh, swiping at my short hair, "Yep. They want that to be the climax, right? All of us face down in the snow."

Reece finishes the last plate and sits across from me, pushing the chair out. "I suppose, but so much has happened since then."

"I hate those articles with the picture of me holding an Orthodox cross. I look so fat."

"But you're gorgeous."

"Right. A gorgeous whale."

"No, you're damn perfect. I love the way your breasts curve up. Beautiful for sure."

"Well, thanks. Are you typing today?" I put my chin in my hands, elbows on the table.

We discuss the changes at Organon. The hospital rooms on the medical unit have been converted to small en-suites for parents and the long-term beds for returned girls. The rooms are filled with returnees, being interviewed and evaluated by Dr. Markush, Dr. Mumford, and a team of four nurses. Reece and I work there four hours a day during the week. It's so strange to see these adults who were snatched by Dahlia, leaving comatose bodies behind. After being released from Dogtown, having failed to find their daughters, they awoke dazed and confused, many in nursing homes and some at home.

We also discuss Julia, praising her goodness. She has ceased interrupting TV programs, but her influence is growing. The first JuliaCon is set for the first week in August. Reece, Arthur, Afewerki, Dr. Markush, and I will be there, plus the other Reece and Emma with whom we had the double wedding. The other Emma walks without a cane now, but her speech is still slow at times.

"What's the latest on Dahlia and Kristin?" I say.

Reece sees them every day, and sometimes Mia spends the day with us. He tells me that Dahlia has calmed down somewhat but is increasingly angry about Julia and her good deeds. Dahlia makes an armadillo appear, but Julia is there to take care of any mayhem. She can transport herself anywhere on Earth, but seems stuck to our planet. She is never gone too long, always craving Kristin's attention.

We go over the events following our return from Gwar. How we had been held prisoners at Organon, or so we thought, Reece's escape and capture, and then the media going crazy for our stories. I remind him of the Reece I had worked with in Gwar. That Reece looks like the one I married, but is about twenty years younger than he is. Reece thinks that I would like a younger, more flexible Reece. The fluorescent ceiling light hums, casting a vibrating light.

"We on for a movie tonight with Arthur?" Reece nudges me under the table and smiles.

We are on, and I decide to type on the back porch, although it's chilly outside.

ORGANON

Markush and Mumford remain busy interviewing the returnees inside the remodeled complex. The beds stay full of returned parents and daughters, most staying about a week. It's noon, and Reece and I are on scene to help with lunch and generally interact with the returnees.

One of the most interesting patients is Alicia Mentone. Her father, Freddie, was a patient at Organon at the same time as the Reeces. Reece found Alicia in an alternate Ethiopia and sent her back with the help of the Abba Paulos. Freddie is staying in the group facility where we spent our first months at Organon. Reece and I have been trained to administer tests to the returnees, the MMPI and inventories for depression and anxiety. Markush is also planning to test for PTSD, which many of the returnees exhibit.

Ever since landing in Reece's backyard, life has been a whirlwind at times. I've stopped doing media interviews and am focusing on my relationship with Reece. He loves me to death, but I still think about the Reece I worked with in Gwar, another planet, perhaps another universe. I wonder if he is still working in Gwar and still mystified at my disappearance. Even though I'm married to Reece, I want to go back to my planet Earth and at least visit. My family and friends are there, and I miss them dearly, even though Reece treats me like a queen.

The returnees move about freely, gathering in the dayroom to play cards and board games. I see Reece through the glass join a small group as I head to the long-term unit to visit with Alicia and her dad. I pass through the door between the units and enter the nursing station. I have a clipboard with questions to ask. Sheila, with the cat-eye glasses, says hey and continues charting. I can see into the rooms through a bank of video monitors. Alicia and her dad, Freddie, are playing ping-pong in the dayroom on perhaps the most expensive ping-pong table ever built.

"Hi, Alicia and Freddie." They stop playing and nod at me. They're bored for now, as most of the residents are. "I'll watch and then have some questions to go over with you."

"Damn, we'll take a break. We've been goofing around," says Freddie. He's thirty-six, short, balding, and sports large red ears that seem to glow beneath his mullet.

We take chairs. "These questions are being asked of everyone here."

"Like a test?" asks Alicia. "I don't like tests." She looks cute in a pair of purple overalls.

"Not a test, just some questions. There are no wrong answers, so no worries." Doing this work makes me feel useful.

"Fire away," says Freddie.

"Okay, first question. Do you currently feel accepted by your community?" I ready my pen for the answers.

"What's my community?" asks Alicia. Her legs dangle, her shoes brushing the floor.

Freddie jumps in. "Like, do you feel welcome at your school, in our neighborhood?"

"Oh, some kids still call me alien girl. I don't like it. But I have my best friend Carmen, who believes everything."

I scribble with haste. "Freddie?"

"That's a hard one. With all the PR you guys did on our

behalf, that helped, but we still get negative attention at stores and such. I received death threats at first, but that has gone away. Now, I have these freaks who want to make Alicia some kind of saint because of her experiences with Dahlia. Like she's a prophet or something. I did quit my job at the warehouse, but the Organon stipend keeps us going."

"Wow, you've paid a high price." I watch the veins in his neck bulge as he leans his head back.

"Yeah, right."

"Next question. What is your biggest fear now that you've been reintegrated?"

Without hesitation, Alicia says, "Dahlia. She's mean. She kidnapped me and sent me to these weird places with weird food. I was in a cage at a circus with a giant whale."

"That's so strange, I know, but real. Dahlia can't hurt you anymore. Julia is watching over you."

"Good," she says.

"I worry about Dahlia as well," says Freddie. "But what I worry about most is the long-term effect on Alicia. She's so paranoid at night. I hate to say it, but we let her sleep in our bed on bad nights."

"Got it. Next question. What can Organon do for you to make your life easier?"

"More money is nice," says Freddie with a short laugh. "But really, what can you guys do other than what you're doing? Dahlia seems to be under control, thanks to Julia. My wife and I believe in Julia and her power to do good."

"Yeah, Julia is nice," says Alicia.

Two more patients, a man and a woman, enter the dayroom and start a game of ping-pong. The tap-a-tap is

Emma

mesmerizing, and I wonder what Reece is doing on the other unit. I wonder what my mother is doing on my own planet. And how is Reece coping by himself in the clinic in Gwar, if he's still there?

Freddie slouches in his chair, as if waiting for the next bombshell to hit. "So, what about the mesh that Markush is talking about?"

"The mesh. Yes, he wants to have an X-ray and biopsy done on those who are willing. It's a tiny sample from your scalp, if the X-ray shows the shadow. He would love it if you agreed."

"Markush explained it to me, and I have a vivid memory from when I was a child of being attacked somehow in my bedroom. There was a bright flash of light."

"Dahlia most likely mapped you as a child, placing the mesh to gather information about who her mother is. That's the general story. The five original Returnees, including me, all tested positive. I've had the biopsy, and it's really simple and fast."

"And the mesh just stays there for the rest of my life? Is it dangerous?"

"As far as I know, it's permanent. It seems to be innocuous. I would've never known had I not been caught up in this crazy adventure."

"Daddy, I don't want a bopsy."

"A biopsy?" asks Freddie.

"Yeah, that."

Freddie speaks to me. "I'll do the biopsy, but it's a hard no for Alicia. She's been through enough."

"I get it. No worries at all. She could choose to do it later in life if she wanted." I smile, feeling like a snake charmer, realizing I am part of something wondrous yet disturbing. I'm at peace, though, being with the man I love and knowing that Julia is in charge.

DENVER, COLORADO

JuliaCon, according to Dr. Markush, is the brainchild of Sherri Loveless and Glenelle Lock. The Pentagon, Congress, and the President remain bewildered at the decline of crime and general nastiness but have, over the year, come to accept the reality of the positive connection between Julia and humanity's condition. JuliaCon celebrates "the human spirit and kindness," according to the brochure. It's been months since any of us have traveled for media events, and we're all excited about the trip to Denver. Each of us, including Markush and Mumford, is on a panel to discuss our experiences in relation to Julia and Dahlia. We arrive Wednesday night for the event, which will last through Saturday evening. Markush briefed us on the plane about safety, as there will be demonstrators, but the world seems to be in a state that would preclude violence, so Reece and I are not worried. He also mentioned a surprise event on Friday evening that would stun the world, but refused to give details.

The Colorado Convention Center resembles an airport, with its massive glass façade facing the street. There are dozens of meeting rooms, a vast ballroom, and an expansive exhibit floor with people hawking everything from t-shirts to books to spiritual guidance. The ongoing panels feature experts on religion, economics, law and order, psychology, and even physics. We are honoring Julia, but Dahlia herself is the star attraction, held tightly by the hand of Kristin, cameras flashing.

We're in suites at the hotel across the street. A cop with

a pistol guards Dahlia's room with Kristin and Markush, but that seems unnecessary. The other Reece and Emma are here too, on the same floor as Reece and me. It's weird to watch them hug and cuddle, as if watching myself with "another" man, although it's essentially the same Reece. In the confusion, Reece was duplicated, and so now there are two. One for me and one for the other Emma.

"Hey, dummy," I say. Reece is tangled in the sheets. "Rise and shine, little squirrel!" I take a feather pillow and hit him on the face.

"Uh, oh, hey, stop," he says, fending me off with an arm.

The suite is spacious, featuring a living room and a compact kitchen. The carpet is a deep red with gray stripes, and the curtains are an inch thick. Last night, after dinner at a steakhouse where Dahlia surprised us by smoking a cigar, we sampled some of the little bottles from the in-room bar. They're eight bucks apiece, but our expenses are covered, so why not?

I playfully cover Reece's face with a pillow and pile on top of him. "We have a panel at ten. Have to eat, princess." Room service has already delivered the bacon and eggs, and it's getting cold.

"Okay, damn, getting up, need to shower." He looks me over, knowing he is a lucky man.

"Stay there," I say, and bring him a black-lacquered tray, the plates covered with shiny metal lids. "Watch the coffee and juice." I retrieve my tray and snuggle up next to him, our breakfasts on our laps.

In forty-five minutes, we're ready to go, our hair still wet from showers. The hotel is packed, and we get serious looks. It's kind of like, "Is that who I think it is?" We exit,

Emma

and the sidewalks are crowded with protestors, holding signs, standing peacefully in small groups. One sign says, "Julia, go home!" I fail to see how anyone could deny the power and goodness of Julia. We cross the street and enter the atrium, shiny, vast, and high. Huge mobiles made of shiny metal and ribbons drape down from the ceiling.

"Where the hell is our meeting space?" asks Reece. He's wearing jeans and a plain, maroon, long-sleeve pullover. I'm wearing this yellow dress Reece likes with white socks and hiking boots.

We take the elevator, and right away we're in trouble. It's a large man with a tight collar.

"I know you! You're one of the Reeces and Emmas. Can I shake your hand?" He reaches for Reece's hand, ignoring me.

We reach the fifth floor, and the man follows us like a lost puppy. The crowds part for us, people staring. Our conference room is packed. There's a table and five chairs at the front with a large screen behind. We don't have a PowerPoint or notes. The title of our session is simply "Our Story." The room is loud, like we're inside a washing machine. We see Dr. Markush and wave. I'm pretty nervous and whisper loudly to Reece. All seats are filled, and people are standing, staring at us. A minute passes, the doors close, and a moderator picks up a microphone and introduces us as "travelers to unknown places" and, surprisingly, "favorites of Julia." The people, all with lanyard nametags, applaud, some whistling. We introduce ourselves, and Reece takes the lead. He recounts the story of Mia being abducted and replaced, and his journey to find her. He's speaking forcefully and a bit loud into the microphone. My stomach flutters as my time to speak approaches. He describes the day Dahlia attacked us in Gwar, our miraculous escape, and our return to this world. Now, it's my turn.

"Hey, I'm Emma Smith, and as you know, I'm married to Reece here." My voice sounds funny, and I wonder if my words make sense. "We've been through a lot, let me tell you." I describe how Reece and I had fallen for each other as we waited for Organon to sort out our lives. I can't help but tell a couple of Dahlia stories and then put Julia on the table. The crowd seems to get extra quiet, straining for my words. My message is that Julia is here to stay and that the world is a better place, which results in applause. I see Markush give me a thumbs up. Reece is staring into space. In addition to his bipolar disorder, I'm pretty sure he's ADD. I end by saying that Julia truly cares for us and that we should recognize her as an omniscient being. We do not have to call her God, but that is essentially who she is. I nod for Reece to take over, and he says, "Thank you," and asks if there are any questions.

Dozens of hands go up. The moderator points to a young woman, wearing jeans and a tie-dye Julia shirt. "What is the best way to pray to Julia?" She folds her arms and blows her bangs.

I laugh at that. "Well, Julia thinks ahead for sure and is always on the lookout for trouble. I don't pray to her as God but more as a friend. Like, 'Hey, Julia, I'm having a bad day. Can you help?' Something like that. You don't have to go to your knees or wear a hair shirt. Just talk, if that makes sense." The moderator points to a man in overalls with ruddy cheeks and a long beard. He stands.

Emma

"My son is a police officer, and he's about to lose his job because of this so-called Julia. What's he gonna do to support his family? Hell, I'm on social security. I can appreciate the fact that crime has decreased, but find it hard to believe that it's all a good thing. My wife and I used to fight all the time, and now it's just plain, like skim milk. This Julia is taking the spice out of life." He sits and gazes around for support.

"I see your son's dilemma," says Reece. "But is it better to have a plain life or a life filled with murder and mayhem? I choose the plain life. However, Emma and I have plenty to disagree about, such as why a trip to Cuba is a good idea for us. I've always wanted to visit, but Emma thinks it's dangerous for some reason. We still bicker, but thank God we get along."

"You gonna give my son a job, you and Julia?" asks the old man.

"Since crime is down, people have been traveling more. That's a whole industry that is expanding. Your son will just have to adapt, I suppose. Mental health is also booming. Chronic disease is waning, but Julia doesn't seem to understand how to cure mental illness, or she chooses not to for some greater good."

The man seems dissatisfied but keeps quiet as the crowd buzzes. The next question comes from a professor-type, wearing an old brown suit coat. He meets my expectations. "I teach college physics, and I've noticed, and my colleagues as well, that students are making better grades, and graduation rates will increase. Is Julia helping students make better grades? Is that a problem?"

Reece nudges me. "Gosh, I don't know. I think Julia

wants everyone to do well, and she kind of composes beneficial situations. I don't think Julia gives answers to tests or writes papers for students. We still have to work for what we want."

"Look," says Reece, "the world is forever changed. Julia is working overtime to save lives and make people happy. It's our duty as human beings to embrace the goodness and multiply the fruits of our good fortune."

I look at Reece as he speaks, admiring his answer.

Days are busy attending sessions and wandering the vast exhibit hall. I buy a Julia bobble-head doll to give to Mia as a birthday gift and a Bible for Reece. The Bible has had all references to God changed to Dahlia. It seems the idea of God in the Bible is closer to a mean Dahlia than to a good Julia. There have been Senate and Congressional hearings that support that idea, seeing Julia as problematic for the economy. Prisons are emptying and not being filled again. Police are bored to tears and being furloughed or taking early retirement. I read that animal shelters are having trouble keeping pets for adoption and have begun to charge exorbitant fees for cats and dogs. The stock market is down, but I don't understand why.

Friday evening rolls around, and we wonder about the surprise Markush mentioned. On the program is "Signature Event, tickets required." It is being held in the Belco Theatre within the complex, which has five thousand seats. I'm dressed in all blue, and Reece wears his usual jeans and a sweater. It's cold in the convention center, but very warm outside.

"Can't wait to see what Dr. Markush has up his sleeve,"

says Reece. He walks briskly, his head slightly bowed.

"Yeah, right," I say. "I just hope no one gets hurt."

We have front row seats, and Arthur, Afewerki, Kristin, Mia, and Dahlia are there. The other Reece and Emma are nowhere to be found. Armed guards linger at the sides to keep order, I suppose. We all greet each other and take our seats to see the show. I sit beside Arthur.

"You are looking lovely as always," says Arthur to me.

"And you're looking snappy in that wool sweater." He pats my hand.

I stare at the stage, which is broad and empty save a wooden table and a wooden chest. We chat back and forth, waiting, and soon the lights brighten and Markush walks onstage, wearing a blazer and black jeans. The crowd takes a minute to go quiet as he taps the microphone. I glance at Dahlia two seats down, and she's gripping the armrests and swinging her feet.

"I hope something crazy happens," says Reece.

"Welcome to JuliaCon!" says Markush. There is a brief crowd murmur. "This week, we have been celebrating Julia, who has done so many good things for our planet."

Dahlia, I notice, is frowning.

Markush continues speaking. "Serious crime is virtually non-existent. Deaths from heart attacks and strokes have nearly disappeared. Worldwide reports of deadly diseases such as malaria and polio have virtually ceased. I see the good. I feel the good. For the first five billion years of Earth's existence, traditional Gods have ruled. But now we know that the entity that brought us to our pre-Julia exposure was Dahlia, and she is here with us tonight, a seven-year-old girl who has found her mother." The crowd rumbles and hoots. "We have a special guest that you will now meet. In this world and others, he has been instrumental in helping parents recover their abducted daughters. He comes to us from a rural village in Ethiopia. We are hoping to astound you. Welcome, the Abba Paulos."

The crowd applauds, then goes silent. A thin man dressed in a golden robe with a matching skullcap appears from backstage and takes his place behind the wooden platform that looks like it could bear a casket. I tap Reece's arm and point to Dahlia. Her eyes are wide as saucers.

The Abba mutters something as he opens the chest and pulls out a thick vest that looks like it's covered with gems. He slides it over his torso and then raises his arms. He is speaking louder now, but in Ge'ez, his voice steady and pleading. A great wash of electricity fills the auditorium, and the lights go out. There is a scream. A blinding light and the sound of a train. I keep my eyes open with difficulty and grip Reece's arm. A spotlight comes on, and there it is, the Ark of the Covenant with the two angels on top. There is lightning between the wings and something like smoke. Then there is a glowing light surrounded by a corona of flame that rises above the Ark and grows larger, to like twenty feet across. Dahlia is standing with Kristin's hand on her shoulder. The Abba is on his knees, head down.

"Hello," says a girl's voice. The voice is calming.

The bright sphere of light scrambles, and Julia's face appears. She looks like Dahlia, with golden hair and brown skin. There is dead silence, and I wouldn't be surprised if someone faints.

"Hello, people. It's just me, Julia. I've been invited to

answer some questions. It makes me really happy to see everyone coming to this event to celebrate good things. I hope that you're having a good time."

Julia is just there but somehow feels a million miles away. She has such bright and kind eyes, unlike Dahlia's. I can feel the air conditioning. Reece is glued to the image, and Dahlia is standing stock-still. Julia's eyes pan the packed house, as if looking for the tiniest bit of pain. My heart beats like a two-stroke engine.

"Is there a heaven?" asks Julia. "So many of you want to know that. Well, there is no heaven as you've learned about. There are no streets of gold. What there is is called the Pinch. Your perfect idea lives there with me every day. From your idea are an infinite number of real-life examples that live among the universes. When you die, your body turns to dust, and your essence returns to that perfect idea. But it's a peaceful place that you will like until the next you is sent out into the universes."

"Hey!" shouted Dahlia. The image of Julia briefly blurs. "That was my idea, sister! Not yours!" There is a gasp as Dahlia towers up high to be face-to-face with Julia. "Go back where you belong, sister. These people don't need you."

An arm extends from the flaming circle, and a hand gently pushes Dahlia back down to size. "So, next question. Are your sacred scriptures true? In a way, I would say, but you have to see them as stories that try to get at what goodness is. Dahlia chose to be hateful, and so you have a hateful world. You want to believe that God cares for you, but also that He will punish you if you're bad. Many of your people follow the example of Jesus Christ, who was a good man. The world needed and still needs a Jesus or a Muhammad, but they were only human, just like you. Since Dahlia was so careless, you had to come up with something to make you feel better." The silence continues, only broken by coughs.

"Question three: Why are people so greedy? I ask myself that all day long, but it's quite simple. Some people are rich and some are poor, but most are in between. That makes people greedy, seeing all the things that other people have. Whether they know it or not, I'm working with your leaders to correct the greed problem. Greed is dirty."

Julia goes silent for half a minute. Suddenly, the theatre is filled with cicadas. They are thick as bees, getting into my hair. Reece is shielding me. Arthur remains seated, slashing the air with his big paws. Afewerki is standing with his arms wrapped around his head. Kristin is yelling. A general panic ensues, but there is a flash of light, and the bugs disappear. The audience is a mess, many on the floor and in the aisles.

"Dahlia still tries, but I have my eye on you, sister," says Julia, and she yawns.

MULDRAUGH

On Sunday, we arrive by private jet back to Louisville and then take a military van to the base. Kristin needs a break from the kids, so they are coming for a sleepover. Dahlia seems so docile lately and less focused on mayhem. It's almost as if she is depressed. The doorbell rings, and I drop the cat, who has been purring in my arms.
"Hey, guys!" I say.
Dahlia clings to Kristin as Mia runs into the house. Reece comes down the stairs and says hey.
"Mommy, don't leave me," says Dahlia. She looks like an adult in her blue, pleated short pants and yellow t-shirt.
"Honey, it's just for the night. I need to get some rest, okay? You can call me whenever you want." Kristin's thin face looked strained.
"No!"
"Yes, Dahlia. Go see what Mia is doing. I think she went out back to see the dog," I say.
It takes another five minutes of pleading from Dahlia before Kristin can leave. Surprisingly, I get Dahlia interested in a puzzle. As I watch, the pieces of the puzzle assemble themselves, and it's finished within minutes.
"I'm bored." Dahlia sits at the kitchen table, her arms crossed and her legs dangling.
I check in with Reece, who is out back with Mia. We decide to play Frisbee in the front yard and gather behind the trees that line the road. A passing car honks, and we wave as usual, not knowing who is honking. Dahlia throws the Frisbee with precision, but is not very strong, so we

make the circle smaller. Mia seems to be having fun. After Frisbee, the girls watch some TV, while Reece and I cook fried chicken with mashed potatoes and green beans. I often think of how spicy the food was in Ethiopia, and my scalp starts to tingle.

"Emma!"

It's Mia, and I walk to the living room. "What's up? Dinner will be ready in half an hour."

"Dahlia's being nasty. She says I came out of mommy's pussy hole."

"Well, she did," says Dahlia. She's grim and not enjoying herself.

"You're jealous!" says Mia.

"I'll put you back in a cage at the circus!" says Dahlia.

"You need to be in a cage!"

"Girls, settle down. Dahlia, that's not a nice thing you said."

"Well, too bad, sister."

"Just watch some more *Scooby Doo,* please, and try not to fight, okay?" I can see how Kristin is so tired and rejoin Reece in the kitchen.

"Dahlia's got the potty mouth going," I say.

Reece laughs as he turns the chicken, which spatters on the marigold stove. The house, built in the 1930s, was updated in the 1960s and seems like a time capsule. He checks his cell phone.

"Who's texting?" I say.

Reece hesitates.

"Who?"

"I didn't want to say anything, but the Emma who lives in Alabama, the one who saved my life, has been texting

Emma

me. She wants to meet."

"What? And you texted her back?" I'm upset and can feel the presence of this other Emma in the room. "What does she want?"

"I don't know. I thought she was married, but she's divorced now."

"Holy cow! She's got her sights on you. Do not text her back, okay?"

Reece closes his phone with a dismal look. This other Emma is Reece's age and has a connection with him that I don't have. I'm not happy at all.

"No, no, all is well. She's just curious. She wants to meet up and talk."

"You're going to meet her? When? Where?" This is just going too far.

"I don't know, soon? You're welcome to join us so you can see there's no hanky panky."

"Hanky panky! I didn't even mention that. Is that what you want, hanky panky?"

"No! She just wants to talk. Chicken is done." He grabs the thighs from the iron skillet and places them on paper towels.

"No more texting with her, got it."

"Okay, but we will meet, and you will go with me, so there."

"Ugh, you make me so mad." I go into frenzy mode and set the table in record time. "Girls! Dinner is ready!"

Dahlia and Mia join us and take their places, each frowning. Dahlia makes her green beans float in the air, and she catches them with her mouth. It's amusing and disturbing at the same time. We muddle through dinner,

Reece and I not speaking.

After dinner, Reece washes up, and we get ready to watch TV together. The girls are playing in Mia's room. There was a presidential press conference earlier in the day, and we're getting the recap. The government is accepting both Dahlia and Julia, but has taken the position that Dahlia is best for the economy. The judicial and criminal systems are collapsing, and jobs are being lost. Retail shopping is down. Home sales are down. Banks are doing okay, as people are saving more money, although they are borrowing less. Placing faith in Dahlia is a colossal mistake, I think, and Reece agrees. The local church we've been visiting, a Baptist church, has adopted Julia into their teachings. We still use the Bible, though.

My mouth is still greasy from the fried chicken, and I lean over and give Reece a big kiss. I really love him, despite the age difference. I think the universes have aligned for us to be together, but I'm pissed that Reece is texting with the Alabama Emma. She had her turn, and Reece chose Kristin.

Funeral homes are declaring bankruptcy, but the baby industry has been booming. In one of her TV broadcasts a few months ago, Julia said that all humans have been given a life expectancy of one hundred. As a result, the CDC has predicted an unprecedented population increase. I'm excited to live so long, but Reece has his reservations, saying that old age is not a party.

Reece checks on the girls, and they have moved outside in the backyard with the dog, Rupert. It's getting dark, and he tells them to come inside. Dahlia protests, and Reece lets them take Rupert into the guest bedroom. Rupert is a spotted mutt with a long, skinny tail. Thankfully, he has the patience of Job. Reece and I settle back onto the fake-leather couch, his arm and leg draped over me. He's flipping channels and finds a movie in progress. Seems like a rom-com. It doesn't matter what we watch as long as we're together. He pinches my thigh.

"Hey!"

"You're so cute. I couldn't resist."

I lean in and kiss him. He pushes into me and returns the favor. I twist and turn, and soon he is on top of me, his hands roaming freely. I worry about the girls, but I'm feeling good. Reece sits up and takes off his shirt. His shoulders are broad, and his chest hairy in the middle. He has this one spot on his back that he loves to be scratched until it bleeds. We go sideways, knocking pillows to the floor, when Dahlia appears.

"Carnal knowledge!" says Dahlia. "Shame on you! You better behave, you psychos. Making a baby so it can suffer."

We scramble into respectable positions.

"We were wrestling," says Reece with a blank look. His hair is all wonky, and he briefly looks like a little boy.

"Ha! Liar!" She takes a seat on the oversized love seat.

"Dahlia, what is love?" asks Reece.

Dahlia sits up straight. "Love is bullshit, my good fellow, and sex is disgusting, but I love my mommy."

"Wow," I say. "Reece and I love each other like you love Kristin. That's okay, right?"

"Yeah, but we don't play tonsil hockey and all that crap."

"You're learning, I think," says Reece. "When you get older, if you can get older, you'll understand." He squeezes me with his arm and kisses my forehead.

"Oh no, I'm getting older. I really hadn't thought about that. That really sucks. Julia stays the same, and I turn into an old witch."

"You're human now, I think," says Reece.

"Ugh, that's disgusting." Dahlia yawns and jumps at the sound of Mia yelling from the bedroom.

ORGANON

A week has passed, and Reece and I still work mornings at Organon. It's strange to meet these people whom Dahlia wronged, their daughters whisked away to other planets, other universes. There are thousands of these parents, and Markush is developing a more effective process to debrief and test them. We only have twelve beds on each unit, and the patients stay for three days, all getting the head X-ray and biopsy. So far, everyone is positive for the mesh, which is mainly made of thallium cuprate.

The government's stance on Dahlia as the "best God" has created waves. Protests have resumed between the two camps, without violence so far, but the conflict is definitely there. Supporters of Dahlia have been galvanized by the Truth Ranch in California, led by Simon Klinefelter, an ex-Mormon. Julia, I think, has the upper hand, though, assimilating those who worship a traditional God. The Reverend Clarity Stillwell and the Christian Instinct Network have recognized Julia as a "good being." Even the Girl Scouts have incorporated Julia into their program, using her image at cookie sales. Reece says it's the status quo versus change, which people fear, even though life has improved with Julia.

Mia and Dahlia are back in school, and Kristin is relieved. She's been measuring Dahlia, and Dahlia has grown an inch. She gave up her supernatural state to be human and have a mother. Her powers seem to be diminishing, as if a battery is being drained of its force.

Those who support Dahlia have designated Kristin as a

godly figure, Christlike. She certainly has the patience of Job, but the strain is too much at times, and Markush has prescribed an antidepressant. Both Reece and I, and the other original Returnees, have been aggrandized as spiritual leaders of Julia. We get tons of requests for interviews, but I've said all I can. Julia is real, and she's the hope of the future.

Arthur rides back with us after work, and we're headed to the Ritz diner for a late lunch. Inside is warm like bread, and our server is sweating. She's the waitress with the big hips and a delicate mustache. Her nametag says "Donna," and we order.

"Thank you for the excursion," says Arthur. He's wearing a wool sweater despite the heat. "I get lonely in the guest house."

"We need to find you a lady friend," I say.

"Yeah, you're famous. You can have your pick, my friend," says Reece.

"It's odd that I have been thinking about that very issue. There was a lady who helped Reece and me find Mia. Reece, you remember her, Caroline Marquette, the woman I pushed who had the audacity to sue me."

"Yeah, she was helpful but a handful, a real dame in distress. I wonder what happened to her?" asks Reece.

"Is she pretty?" I say. Arthur seems so timeworn, like a statue with chiseled facial features.

"Against my better judgment, yes, she is attractive. I think about her often."

"Maybe she's lost," I say. "Like the Reece I worked with at the clinic. I wonder what happened to him? I think that in the shuffle, he was lost too."

"Here comes the missing Reece again," says Reece. He's jealous of that Reece and self-conscious about being older than I am.

I speak. "We worked hard together, just like you did in your clinic with an Emma, who has been texting you, by the way."

I'm not at all happy about this other Emma, especially since she saved Reece's life when he was shot.

"You have found each other, and that is enough," says Arthur. "I was delighted when you married."

"We have it good," I say, as Donna brings our food, one plate at a time. It looks hot and greasy.

"If it weren't for the chromosomal differences, we would've had a baby by now," says Reece.

"Yes, the chromosomes. I believe I understand now that we have DNA, which harbors these chromosomes. The chromosomes instruct the human form as to its appearance and function. I am learning so much that it boggles the mind. I've been reading philosophers who existed beyond my original state, such as Husserl and Sartre. It's quite surprising, the darkness that my idealistic forms have rendered."

"Not surprising with all those years of Dahlia at the helm," says Reece, who taught philosophy prior to Organon. "It should be darker than it is."

The diner bustles with several newcomers spacing themselves out in the maroon, upholstered booths. There's grit, a dead fly, and a few hairs occupying the windowsill. I gaze at Arthur and Reece. We are all beings from different planets, possibly from other universes. The circumstances that led us here to this diner at this time are incomprehensible. I have to catch my breath in wonder.

"Positivism and empirical proofs seem to be things rusted and useless," says Arthur.

I'm not sure what he is talking about, but Reece chimes in, and I let them hash it out while I tackle my catfish and butterbeans.

"It's a new world with Julia," says Reece. "We need a new philosophy of life and its exigency."

"Julia works wonders, it is true, but she has taken to what you call micromanagement, I fear." Arthur puts his chin in his hand. He looks regal and relaxed. "Humanity is making choices that lead to good outcomes, but there seems to be no heart in it. I'm craving a bit of bad news myself. Surely someone wants to rob a bank, but they are restrained by Julia."

"Yeah," I say. "It all seems great but contrived. I wonder how long Julia can keep up her watch? She's so involved and busy." I watch an ant crawl up the window.

"As long as she can take it," says Reece. "It's only been a year or so since Dahlia vacated her pristine throne. Anything can happen at this point, but I feel there will be a breaking point."

I agree with Reece and wipe ketchup from his sleeve.

FORT KNOX

A few months have passed, and it's damn cold. There's three inches of snow on the ground and icicles hanging from the gutters. Reece says the gutters need cleaning, but is waiting for spring to roll around. Meanwhile, the world is in an uproar over Julia versus Dahlia. The United States is just about split, with states making official declarations of recognition. In Africa, there have been great revivals celebrating both Julia and Dahlia. Europe is under the spell of Julia, with Denmark leading the charge to make Julia the official God. The Middle East is torn like the United States between a traditional God and Dahlia or Julia. To me and Reece, it's a matter of what is versus what was.

A surprising development is the return of some petty crimes, such as robberies. The victims, thus far, all retaliated and in one case shot their perp. Julia is allowing this to happen. Reece says she's getting tired and maybe a little lazy, which I hope isn't true. At the PX, in the parking lot the other day, a woman opened her car door and hit my car pretty hard. I expected her to apologize, but she accused me of parking too close. The relentless niceness is just not there anymore. It's as if people have been pretending and are tired of being good. It's interesting that TV crime shows are really popular now, as if people are craving some badness in their lives.

Afewerki has passed his TOEFL exam and has mainstreamed into a major in criminal justice. We enjoyed having him for a couple of days during the holiday break. He seems happy, but often talks about his family. He's like me in wondering if the Abba Paulos could send us back. I love Reece and my life, but this is not my true home. It doesn't help that the Alabama Emma keeps contacting Reece, and Reece always responds. He's dying to meet up with her, but I've said no way.

Arthur is doing well, reading and writing. He goes on walks around the lake, mumbling to himself and chatting up anyone he meets. Caroline Marquette weighs heavy on him, and he wishes to find her. I think he has the hots for her despite her being an enemy for the latter part of his life in his world.

We talk to Markush just about every day. He, Kristin, Mia, and Dahlia have moved into his house in Radcliff. He stays busy with the returnees at Organon and traveling to D.C. He's all about promoting Julia and learning as much as he can about her. He talks with her at length, assuming that she hears him. All the returnees thus far have the mesh. One patient, an older gentleman, allowed Markush to remove a section of mesh versus just a biopsy. Markush says that researchers at a lab in D.C. are working to interface with the mesh, which is microfine and packed with information that Dahlia gathered.

The other Reece and Emma, we don't see them that often, except at work. They tend to work in the afternoon, and Reece and I in the morning. Honestly, it's like looking in the mirror when we're together. Markush endlessly confuses us, as do the others at Organon, and begs us to get different haircuts. The Reeces have receding hairlines with not much to work with. The back of Reece's hair grows much faster than the front, and I occasionally trim the back.

Emma

Reece comes inside after raking leaves. "Had another sign in the yard."

"Which one?"

"Julia, So Sweet." He heads into the kitchen for a Gatorade.

The sign has come to mean an insult to Julia and her followers. These days, feelings run strong, and they seem to be running strong between Dahlia and Julia as well. Kristin has become very protective of Dahlia and is now more of a gatekeeper than a mother. Things have gotten cool between Kristin and Markush, and they argue about how to handle Dahlia. Reece thinks they are headed for a split, and I'm worried that Kristin might try to draw Reece back into her arms.

All of the original Returnees, including me, have been offered book deals. Arthur has already published an article in a prestigious philosophy journal. Strangely, West Coast publishers want to tie in our stories with Julia, and East Coast publishers stress Dahlia. Although we're comfortable, thanks to Organon, the $250,000 advance I was offered would be very welcome. I've discussed the book thing with Sherri Loveless, and she says that I should negotiate for twice what I'm being offered.

Outside, it's thirty degrees and overcast. A roast is in the crockpot, and there is corn on the cob and yeast rolls. I like our big kitchen with its high ceilings. The linoleum is worn, and the cabinets are dated, but we love eating at the farm table. I put placemats on the table, which Reece finds unnecessary. If I let him place the silverware, he always gives me a small fork, which upsets me more than it should. He does it on purpose to get the reaction.

"Dinner's ready!" I call out to the room, to the house, to the entire planet. I hear him coming down the stairs.

"No need to shout!" Of course, he shouts that.

"Getting cold!" I'm egging him on.

He steps through the pantry into the kitchen, still wearing his green wool coat that Kristin's parents gave him a dozen years ago. We keep the house at 68 degrees in winter, but we both stay cold and wear layers in the house.

"My parents used to shout from room to room, and it always pissed me off," says Reece.

"So, I piss you off?"

"This looks great, dearest darling. And *it* pisses me off, but not *you*."

"Well, thanks, I suppose. We still going to see your grandparents?" After Reece's parents were shot in Texas, his grandparents took him in. He more or less worships them. Dora is about seventy, and Horace is ten years her senior. He likes to say he robbed the cradle, and always with a smile. They're good country people who moved to the big city looking for a better life. Horace is retired from a pipe shop in Birmingham and spends most of his time gardening and reading. When he salts his food, the salt goes everywhere. I love Horace and Dora too. Her eyes sparkle when Reece is around.

Reece takes a swallow of sweet tea. "Yes, still going on Saturday. Kristin wants us to take Mia, which is great. They haven't seen Mia in a while."

"That sounds good. What's up with Dahlia?"

Reece leans back in his chair, which he knows I don't like. "I don't know, man. Kristin is changing from a reluctant mother to somewhat of a bulldog. She takes Dahlia

Emma

very seriously and is definitely on her side of things. Mia is just an appendage these days. I feel bad for her. I think if I asked for custody, Kristin wouldn't bat an eye."

"We've talked about that, taking in Mia. I would be up for it. Mia adores you, and she's just being brainwashed by Kristin." A cold wind blows over and around the house, making a low moan.

"Yeah, it's on the table," says Reece. "I don't want Mia to be neglected and live in the shadow of a former God who is basically a bully. The more I think about it, it just can't be healthy for her."

"Have you noticed, though, how quiet Dahlia is lately? It's like she's waiting for something. She kind of gives me the creeps."

"Something's up, I'm sure."

We finish eating, taking our time. We don't have a dishwasher, but Reece likes to wash dishes, and he does that, letting them dry in the rack. I check the fridge and we're good for a couple of days, except for orange juice, which Reece drinks straight from the bottle when I'm not looking.

We retire to the living room to watch an episode of *X-Files*. The episodes are always mysterious and sometimes supernatural, but nothing can compare with the bizarre reality of what we have been through. It's so strange to see crimes committed when crime is a thing of the past, or so we hope. The supporters of Dahlia harp on the need for evil to make good stand in sharper relief. I like the approach of our church to accept Julia as a divine helper who holds the keys to human happiness. We still pray to God and study the Bible, but with a new slant. There are the Julia purists, though, who preach the infinite goodness and power of Julia alone.

Reece puts his arm around me and pulls me close. He doesn't bathe every day like I do, but he never smells bad. Sometimes, like tonight, he smells of potatoes. A commercial for a diabetes monitor plays. I know what Reece will do next. He grabs my legs and places them across his lap, and then leans over. He wants me to scratch his back.

"Okay, buster," I say. I yank up his shirt and begin scratching long and hard.

"Ooh," he says, twisting this way and that to get my fingers where they need to be.

"You lucky boy." I dig deeper and go faster until he yelps.

"It's okay, keep going," he says. Another gust of wind hits the house, and leaves swirl in the front yard. The piles Reece has made scatter, and some scrape the window.

I know it's a bad time to mention, but I do it anyway. "Has that Emma texted you again?" I slow my scratching, and when he does not respond, I stop. "Huh, so she has?" I pull his shirt down, and he sits up with a wan look on his face.

"Thank you, thank you. That was so good."

"You didn't answer my question."

He puts his head in his hands and mumbles.

"What?"

"Yes, she has. She wants to meet, just have a conversation."

"Really? Have you agreed to meet her?" I squeeze his thigh hard.

"Hey now." He pauses. "The answer is yes. We are going

to meet and you're going with me. How about that?" He folds his arms and looks me in the eyes.

"Why would I want to meet her? I don't know her. She saved your life and now she wants the rewards, right?"

"Look, she's an important facet of my life. I owe her a visit, and you guys should meet. She's older than you are and probably looks like a horse by now." He tries to laugh,

"Oh, I'll look like a horse when I get older?" He's not doing well.

"No, no. She just can't be more attractive than you are."

"You're with me just because of looks? We share a bond. We went through something together that this other Emma can't even approach."

"But she saved my life, right? Would you rather I see her alone?"

I think about that. Maybe it's smarter to go along and show the other Emma what love looks like. "Okay, I'll go with you." I speak with definite anger, but can't see a better way out.

I'm pretty sure that he's already set a date to see her, but he "supposes" he will get with her and make plans. I tell him to do that and let me know exactly when and where they will meet.

"Yeah, sure, no worries," he says.

ALABAMA

Kristin broke up with Markush and moved back to the safety of the guest house. She is becoming more and more protective of Dahlia each day. She has developed this stern look, as if she is in great danger. Markush is devastated, but what can he do? He spends his days working with the returnees at Organon and takes frequent trips to D.C. He wants to fully diagram Dahlia's DNA, but Kristin says no. Dahlia seems to take Kristin's paranoia as love. They more or less cling to one another, as if fate should tear them apart.

It's Saturday and still cold. The snow has mostly melted, but the skies glow a dull white as if more is on the way. Reece and I are driving to Alabama, first to see the amazing Emma, and then we'll go visit Reece's grandparents and spend the night. We pick up Mia at Kristin's request, and Mia is pleased to see us. I feel bad for Mia, Kristin playing obvious favorites with Dahlia. Dahlia has possessed her.

The drive to Hueytown takes about six hours with a bathroom break for Mia and then some fast food. Once there, he knows exactly how to get to Emma's house. We pull into a long driveway. The house is two stories with a large carport. Flowers line the driveway and the front of the house. The largest Hosta I've ever seen sits inside a ring of pinkish rock. Leaves cover the lawn.

"You okay?" asks Reece.

"No." I'm nervous to meet her, imagining they'll hit it off like old times.

He doesn't hold my hand or put his arm around me,

Emma

and knocks on the carport door. Mia stands like a statue. Emma's mom, a woman in her sixties, appears, wearing a fleece vest over a sweatshirt with jeans. She's thin and bony with a wrinkled forehead.

"Well, hey!" she says. "Long time no see!"

She opens the screen door for us, and we walk into a small, dimly lit kitchen that features a yellow stove and fridge.

"My god, you look like Emma when she was in her twenties," she says to me.

"Nice to meet you," I say, my tummy in knots. It's uncanny how she favors my mother, although older. "And this is Mia, Reece's daughter."

"Hi, Mia. You're a cute little thing. Emma!" she shouts as she leads us into a large living room that is sparsely furnished.

I take a seat on the couch, and Reece remains standing with Emma's mom. Mia takes a lone stuffed chair. I'm guessing her name is Betty, like my mom's. Reece and Betty chat away, and I feel left out. Someone is coming down the stairs, and I focus on relaxing. It's her, the famous Emma.

"Reece!" she says, and they hug.

Reece pats her on the back like an old friend. Then they stare at each other for an eternity. I clear my throat.

"Emma, this, of course, is Emma," says Reece.

I stand and stare at an older me. She looks so fresh with rosy cheeks and bouncy, shiny hair. I feel like a plaything. Reece can't take his eyes off her.

"Hi." We shake hands.

"Nice to meet you."

"I'll leave y'all to talk," says Betty, and she disappears

into the kitchen.

We sit awkwardly on the couch with Reece in the middle. I instantly feel left out as Reece is focused on her.

"What have you been up to?" asks Reece. "By the way, this is Mia."

"Hi, Mia!" she says. "Just getting divorced is all. We argued all the time."

"That sucks."

"Yeah, in a major way. But all is as it should be. There's no kids, so that's good." She gives Reece a half-smile, which I know he loves from me. Reece is melting into her, and I can feel it.

Reece then tells the story of how Mia was abducted and how he traveled via seizures to find her. He recounts the day we were returned and then, surprisingly, tells her about our wedding. I'm feeling a little better with Reece acknowledging our history and bond.

"And you have contact with Dahlia herself?" she says.

Reece explains the situation, saying that Kristin and Dahlia have developed a tight bond. To us, Dahlia is just a mischievous little girl, but with a regal history.

"What do you make of Julia?" she says. I notice that she puts her hand on Reece's thigh for a few seconds.

Reece finally looks at me. "She is divine and wants the best for all of us. Have you tried praying to her? She'll do most anything, although of late she seems to be pulling back."

"Actually, I have," she says with a smile, and that makes me wonder what she wished for.

"Good, good. Gosh, it's great to see you, and your mom too," he says.

Emma

"Can I go outside and play?" asks Mia.

Reece asks if it's okay and gives his blessing. I want to go outside too, but not to play. I'm worried about leaving them alone.

As with most outsiders, Emma is interested in Dahlia and Julia. Reece is of the opinion that there is a conflict brewing between the two and that all hell will break loose.

"Can I get y'all something to drink? Momma keeps a pot of coffee on."

It's cool in the house, and both Reece and I take her up on coffee. They continue to talk, and I nod my head as if I'm a part of the conversation. Two hours go by, and Mia is bored. I remind Reece that we're having dinner with his grandparents, and he looks pained. Finally, a half hour later, Reece is ready to go. They hug, and I shake Emma's hand, eager to leave.

In the car, I say, "Thank God that's over."

"Oh, don't be that way," says Reece. "It was great to see her. We'll have to stay in touch. She's part of our weird family."

"Not my weird family."

"I thought she was nice," says Mia. "I didn't have anything to do, though."

It takes an hour, and we arrive at Reece's grandparents' house. They have moved to the heart of Pell City from the lake house that Reece loved so much. The house is built on a foundation of rocks and cement and wrapped with tan vinyl siding. Two massive water oaks tower in the front yard. I'm nervous for sure, not having seen them since the wedding, and still feeling queasy from Reece salivating over the other Emma.

"Do I look okay?" I say.

"Looking good," says Reece. "And Mia is looking good, too."

We walk up the back stairs to the small deck and the back door. Reece knocks and pushes in.

"Hello!" he says.

"Y'all come in!" says Dora. She's fluffing her graying hair with a pick. She looks bigger than Horace, but it's hard to tell with them sitting down. "Emma, you sure look cute today." I nod and notice that I'm blushing.

Dora and Horace are sitting cozy in their recliners in the den beside the kitchen. The den is long and narrow, with a couch where we take a seat. There's a little gas heater on the paneled wall. I can smell something cooking, but can't tell what.

"Come here, Mia," says Horace. He looks solid with his belly and receding hairline.

Mia stands and walks slowly with wide eyes. Horace fumbles in his pocket and pulls out a dollar. "This is from your grandpa. Save half and spend half, and you'll be rich in no time."

Mia says, "Thank you," and hesitates before going in for a hug. She then turns and gives Dora an awkward hug.

"How was the drive?" asks Horace. Old people always want to know how the drive was, as if it's the most crucial part of the journey.

"Good. We just came from Hueytown," says Reece.

"What were you doing there?" Horace jerks his arm, knocking the plastic phone off a stand between the recliners. "Well damn." He's caught in the cord, and the phone is in the trash can.

"He's so clumsy," says Dora with a sly grin. "Mia, you want a sweet? Horace, get her something sweet."

"I'm okay," says Mia.

Horace is already up, grunting. He takes Mia into the kitchen and gives her a Little Debbie oatmeal cream pie. I hear him ask Mia if she likes milk, and she says no. They return, and Horace falls into his recliner like it's a giant beanbag.

"Speaking of driving, I remember one day I was out with Papa in the wagon on an old country dirt road. We pulled around a bend, and lo and behold, there was a baby in the ditch. Naked as a jaybird and covered with mud."

I can tell that Reece has heard this story before, but he pretends. "Was it dead?" he says, holding back a smile.

"Dead as a mackerel." Horace twiddles his thumbs.

I have to ask. "What did you do?"

"Papa put it in a flour sack, and I don't know what happened after that. Life sure can be hard. I don't even know if it was a boy or a girl." He seems like his eyes are misting.

"Dahlia did that," says Mia. She's sitting on the edge of the couch with a blank look.

"Oh Lord, Dahlia," says Dora. "I still don't get why she was so mean. And you've met the rascal."

"She was made that way," says Mia. "Julia wants to fix all the bad things."

"Yeah, Dahlia is a trip," says Reece. "Mean as a snake, but she can't help it and just lets humanity run amok."

"Amok? What does that mean?" asks Dora. I notice she has a word-search puzzle book in her lap.

"Now, Dora, you know what that means," says Horace. "It means crazy." Horace graduated from high school at the age of twenty and loves to read. The small bookcase beside his recliner is filled with *National Geographics*.

"Shut up," says Dora, and I have to laugh, but stop at her next remark. "Emma, you done gained some weight since the wedding. You look healthy. You're not pregnant, are you?" She continues to pick at her hair.

"You're pregnant?" asks Mia.

I choose my words. "No, not pregnant, but definitely healthy."

Reece explains the chromosomal difference.

"My, my," says Dora. "We forget she's from another, uh, planet, I think." She puts down her pick, as if contemplating something beyond her ken.

"What I don't understand is how there are two of you, Reece," says Horace.

"I got duplicated when I was returned. I'm the real deal, and the other Reece is a copy. Some wires got crossed in the transfer, which is the best I can explain."

"Well, we sure are glad to have you back, boy," says Horace. "And glad that everything with Mia has worked out."

"I'm just happy to be alive and have Mia back," says Reece.

"Anything else?" I say.

"And I'm so lucky to have this beautiful Emma by my side." He kisses my cheek.

"What about the other Emma, the one in Hueytown, who's your age and who saved your life?" I can't help myself, still burning from our little visit.

"She's just...part of the family, I suppose. You can't erase history, right?" Reece leans forward and stares at the pink carpet that is worn and dingy in places. "What about the Reece you worked with in the clinic? You have a bond with him."

I have to explain that Reece to his grandparents. I tell them that he got left behind when Reece and I were returned. "He was a younger version of your Reece," I say.

The room goes quiet for a minute as Mia nibbles her oatmeal pie.

ORGANON

The weekend with Reece's grandparents went okay. I just wish that I could forget about this other Emma. It's Monday, and back to the Organon grindstone. Per Kristin's orders, Mia has come to live with us. Kristin is becoming increasingly withdrawn and protective of Dahlia. I would say she is paranoid. After dropping Mia off at school on base, Reece and I head to Organon for our day shift. We're still a full house with about three patients leaving each day and new ones taking their places.

We start by delivering breakfast trays, then administer the various mental health questionnaires. Downtime is spent conversing with various characters, all with the same story of having a daughter abducted and then traveling across universes to find them. In room five on the former medical unit is a guy named Dustin Jeh. He's a regular fellow with brown hair and a habit of sucking through his teeth. Reece and I serve lunch at 11:30, and then we're done for the day, handing over the reins to the other Reece and Emma. Reece and I usually hang out with them for a few minutes before we go. We agree to head over to their place for dinner at six.

Dr. Markush appears, and he looks worried. The government has chosen Dahlia as the reasonable god, which infuriates him. Organon is pro-Julia, and Dahlia is just another little girl with the occasional show of power. He's distraught over the breakup with Kristin and is worried that she's going off the deep end. He gets a call from Glenelle Lock and excuses himself.

Emma

In the past few months, my Reece has been going to the base gym and running around the neighborhood in his black shorts and black sweatshirt. He hates the cold and only runs about a mile three or four times a week. Reece encourages me to exercise, although he says I have a no-maintenance body, meaning I look good without exercise, which is a nice thing to say. I just don't like gyms or running. The base gym that Reece goes to smells like a dirty sock.

At home, I make a coconut pie for dinner. Reece runs to the store for pudding mix and a pie crust. Mia helps me in the kitchen and seems sad. She loves Reece dearly but is very attached to Kristin. I think she feels rejected and misses the drama with Dahlia. I let Mia run the mixer, whipping egg whites and sugar for the topping.

Snow trickles as we drive to Radcliff. Reece and Emma live in a two-bedroom apartment in a quiet neighborhood. The complex has a pool, and we'll be visiting in the summer for sure. I carry the pie, and Reece knocks.

"Welcome, welcome," says the other Reece.

"Thank you, thank you," says my Reece.

"Hi, Reece," says Mia. She's brought her pink backpack and a couple of books. Mia is becoming a real reader.

The living room features all black furniture, giving it a modern look. The Reeces plop down on the couch, and I head to the small kitchen where Emma is cooking. She walks without a cane, and her speech has become clear. She told me that she had been praying to Julia for healing.

"Hey, sister!" I say.

"Hey, yourself," she says with a half-smile. There's meatloaf in the oven, and she's whipping up some mashed potatoes. The kitchen window looks out over a steep hillside.

"How's married life?" I say. "Damn hot in here," and I take off my coat.

"Good, just not making babies is all."

"Yeah, same here. But you still try, right? I know we do, although Reece has gotten a little lazy."

"How many times a week?" she says. She dumps melted butter onto the mashed potatoes and adds sour cream.

"Truthfully, maybe once a week, usually on a Monday for some reason."

"Monday sex? That's weird. I think we're in the same boat, the boys getting bored." She laughs.

"Yeah, we might need to visit a sex store soon," I say.

"But we love each other. That's all that matters," she says. "Is Reece still barking up the tree of that Emma in Alabama? I have to ask." The oven beeps, and she removes the meatloaf, which is covered with ketchup.

I glance into the living room, where Mia is reading and the boys are talking. "He's just so fascinated with her, but maybe in a platonic way? He can't get over the fact that she saved his life when he was shot. They had really bonded, and he almost committed adultery with her."

"He's got to keep his eyes on the prize, which is you. I wouldn't let him see her again. She sounds dangerous." She transfers the potatoes to a serving bowl.

"We'll see. I'm definitely not encouraging him. I don't want to make her the forbidden fruit. Is your Reece toeing the line as they say?"

"Yeah, as far as I know. He gets steamy letters from strangers wanting to connect with the magic, but ignores them. I know that we all get them. I had one guy propose marriage." I laugh, knowing the story.

With the food on the table, a chrome and laminate affair, we take our seats. We talk about this and that. Afewerki is doing well at school, and Arthur stays busy writing and preparing lectures. My Reece mentions that Dr. Ory has been nominated for a Nobel prize for his work on the Tiny Bangs Theory, which supports the existence of Dahlia and Julia. We talk about time as the origin of the universes and end up agreeing that it makes as much sense as the Big Bang did.

"Dang, this was good," says the other Reece. "You can't beat a good meatloaf." I know that for a few years, at the behest of Kristin, he was a vegetarian.

We compliment Emma and her cooking, and then we dig into the coconut pie. Mia has two pieces, and I have to deny her a third, fearing she will throw up. Outside, a cop car whizzes by on the main road with sirens blasting as we filter into the living room. My Reece wants us to see what's on CIN, the Christian Instinct Network, which is broadcasting live tonight from Clarity Stillwell's church in Colorado Springs.

The adults take the couch, and Mia leans back against my legs on the floor. We drop in about five minutes late, and it's Stillwell on the screen. Behind him is a massive choir loft and a large window for the baptismal. He's holding his Bible like a limp lamb and reads from Corinthians 8:6. It's a verse that we all know: "But for us, there is one God, the Father, from whom all things came and for whom we live."

"There is one God, and we worship Him in all his glory!" says Stillwell. He's wearing an off-silver suit with shiny shoes. He looks bulky with narrow shoulders. His blond hair parts on the side, and his black glasses give him a serious look.

"What we have is one lawn but three lawnmowers, but Dahlia and Julia have dull blades and can't master the manicured lawn," says Stillwell.

"What the hell is he talking about?" asks my Reece.

"Got me," I say.

The camera pans to the vast auditorium and a crowd of well-dressed believers. The ceiling is some fifty feet high with large stained-glass windows on the sides.

"God is challenging us by sending these impostors. We must stand strong and fight the true fight." He raises a fist and does a stutter step. The crowd applauds, all with bright faces.

"Bunch of zombies," says the other Reece.

"Damn straight," says Emma.

"What we have is a cake with three candles, and we have to blow out the two that are unleavening our spiritual bread. Are you with me?" A collective "Amen" follows. "At the end of the day, there is no time like the present... to cultivate what we have planted and not that cake which has fallen from the sky."

We all shake our heads and have sly grins. Mia excuses herself to read in a spare bedroom. She's a regular reading machine. Stillwell drones on, and we watch just to be watching.

"All of the good deeds being done in this world are through the one true God." Stillwell straightens his posture and looks toward heaven. "What we need is focus and not to be playing with a barrel of monkeys."

We are in a kind of trance when there is a bright flash of blue light, and Stillwell cowers with one arm over his face. A large shining disk with fire around the edges floats above Stillwell.

"Julia," says my Reece. We all lean forward.

The disk swirls, and then there is the face, the face that looks so much like Dahlia. There are shouts from the audience as the camera seems to wander. Finally, the camera zooms into the vision of Julia, leaving Stillwell off-camera.

"Hi, nice people," says Julia. Her smile is warm. "I just had to drop in. Secretly, many of you have been praying to me, asking for guidance."

"That's a lie!" says Stillwell. The camera zooms out to include him. He's moved to the side of the stage and is looking up. "Get thee behind me, Satan!"

Julia laughs a little-girl laugh. "There is no Satan. Some are saying that Dahlia is Satan. She's just not kind and lets you all do as you please. Human nature is evil, and you need someone to help you make the right choices. Dahlia let you run wild, but I'm here to stop all that."

"This is an outrage!" says Stillwell. He looks tense and small beneath the facsimile of Julia.

"I'm sorry to upset you," says Julia. "But you have to see the truth. You can still worship God, but her name is Julia. Just call my name if you are in trouble, although I'm learning that some of you may deserve to be punished."

"Uh oh, Julia just dropped a bomb," says Emma.

"She can only take so much, I think," says Reece.

The camera pans the audience, and some have stood and moved to the aisles.

"Leave us be, you devil," says Stillwell. "You are a trick of lights, a wolf in sheep's clothing."

"No, I'm for real. Okay, nice people, I will leave now. Be forever kind." The disk poofs out in a flame and flash of light.

Stillwell takes center stage again. "I think we need some music. Brother Tanner, lead us in song."

Tanner rises from his velvet chair and takes position at a podium on the right side of the stage. He chooses an old classic, "Up from the Grave He Arose," and soon, through music, order is restored, and we lose interest. I turn down the volume.

"What a hoot," says Reece.

"Julia is real," I say.

"The truth for sure," says Emma.

ORGANON

Reece and I arrive at Organon at eight a.m. per usual. Everyone is talking about Julia's appearance on TV last night. The patients, as we call them, have a definite bias toward Dahlia and see Julia as the savior. The replay of her little battle with Clarity Stillwell is all over the news. We know that the public face of the current president favors supporting Dahlia as the least problematic solution to the dilemma of who matters most, Dahlia or Julia. Markush, though, tells us that the government, particularly the Pentagon, is fascinated with Julia and wants to establish an official relationship that gives the United States favor in her eyes.

I'm on the former medical unit today, where I help pass out breakfast trays, usually the same: scrambled eggs, sausage, and hashbrowns with juice in little cups. After breakfast, I work on my list of evaluative instruments to give patients. I start in room three with Fred Gantrum. He's showered and ready to hit one of the empty offices where we give the tests. The MMPI takes the longest, about an hour to an hour and a half. The MMPI analyzes personality traits and psychopathology, helping Markush to identify any mental illnesses that may be present, including schizophrenia.

"Here we go," I say, and lead Fred through the locking doors and down a hallway to the office. I explain that the test will ask a series of true or false questions. Fred is thirty-eight and keeps his hair short. He has a great smile, but there's some pain crinkles around his eyes. "Call me on the phone when you're through. Star 9."

I return to the unit and escort another patient to another office in a wheelchair. She had been comatose for nearly six months, while her copy languished in Dogtown. She had been helpless to find her daughter, a seven-year-old named Dee, whom Dahlia whisked away to an Ethiopia somewhere in another universe.

Lunch arrives so soon, and I head to the old long-term unit to meet Reece, where we eat our Organon lunch. Today, it's Salisbury steak, lima beans, and mashed potatoes with a pudding that must be vanilla. We're meeting up with Dr. Mumford to take a walk around the lake before Reece and I head home. From the lobby, we head outside into the frigid air, maybe forty degrees. There's a big spread of melting ice over the lake.

"Round we go," says Reece.

"Gosh, I needed a break," says Mumford. She is a striking figure with her cornrows and model's face. She jokes about being the only black person at Organon, except for a few of the patients.

The trail is graveled and flat but rocky in places. It now goes all the way around when it's not flooded. It's cold, but there's a friendly sun in the sky with tree shadows falling to the north. We scuff through the leaves and chat when Mumford drops a bombshell.

"Did you hear about Kristin?" she says.

"What?" we all say with raised eyebrows.

"Kristin has left with Dahlia and is in California." She looks me in the eye with a look of amazement.

"What?" we say again, and I trip over a rock.

Mumford tells us that Kristin has been communicating

with a character, Simon Klinefelter, from the Truth Ranch in McKittrick, California. He apparently has convinced her that Dahlia is the true God and that she is the royal caretaker. I've seen him on TV, a large man with short, wavy, brown hair and a big belly that droops. He has a thousand-acre ranch where his followers live part-time. They split their time between the ranch and a slaughterhouse that the Ranch owns in Bakersfield.

We all know Kristin was getting somewhat radical, but this news is shocking. She withdrew Dahlia from school and broke up with Markush. The base educational office had been threatening her, saying that Mia had to be enrolled in school or home-schooled.

"Wow," I say. "That Klinefelter guy used to be a polygamist. I wonder if Kristin will become one of his wives?"

"Who knows?" asks Reece. "I lived with her for ten years and would say that she's a strong person, but sometimes too eager to please. I'm just glad she didn't take off with Mia. She's just forgotten Mia, though, and that really hurts her."

"Well, Mia has Emma now, and you. She's loved, so just keep doing that," says Mumford. She looks a bit out of place in her white lab coat over a really nice pantsuit.

"Emma's great with her," says Reece. "She's got that youthful vibe that I seem to be lacking." He laughs.

"Yeah, you're an old man," I say.

"Old man?" he says. "No, just experienced."

"Whatever," I say. There's a moment of silence as we clish-clash through leaves like we're kicking Corn Flakes. Secretly, I've been praying to Julia, asking her to bring the Reece I worked with to the here and now. I just can't forget him and worry that he'll never know what happened to me. I've also been praying that Caroline Marquette be brought here for Arthur. He's lonely and talks about her all the time. Come to think of it, I've been doing a lot of praying to Julia. Last night, I prayed that Afewerki would do well in his studies and somehow find home again. Of course, I miss my home and want to go back, but I have a life with Reece now. I have to remember that. We continue around the lake and tiptoe across mushy ice at one point.

"Reece," says Mumford. "Would you be willing to reach out to Kristin and get as much info as you can?"

"Sure. I can try her cell phone. What do you want me to ask?"

"I think we want to know what her intentions are and if she and Dahlia are safe. The higher-ups are not at all happy, treating it as a security breach."

"When did she leave?" asks Reece.

"Yesterday morning, a flight from Louisville. She arrived there in the afternoon. An unmarked military vehicle followed her to the ranch."

Reece stops. "I can call her right now."

"Maybe wait till you get home. I need to get back to work, admitting two new patients this afternoon, one from Chicago and one from a small town in South Dakota."

"Sure," says Reece. I can see the excitement and worry in his greenish-brown eyes.

"Lots to process," I say.

We continue for another few minutes and reach the trail's beginning. Mumford leaves, and Reece and I jump in the Toyota to pick up Mia from school and then head home to Muldraugh. Traffic is light, and when we enter

Emma

Muldraugh, everything becomes kind of sleepy. I can tell Reece is itching to call Kristin. Maybe this will take his mind off the Alabama Emma.

We pull into the driveway, and I notice someone sitting in a rocking chair on the front porch. I can't believe my eyes.

"Who the hell?" asks Reece.

I'm sure who it is, so I jump out of the car. The person stands as I step up onto the porch.

"Reece!" I say. He's the spitting image of my Reece, but twenty years younger.

"Emma? I have no idea what's going on," he says.

My Reece joins us on the porch. "Reece, it's the Reece I worked with in Gwar, right?"

"Yes, Gwar, but I was caught up in an electrical storm of some sort when you disappeared, and I wound up in Dogtown." This new Reece is thin and looks hungry. "I'm so happy to see you," and we hug.

"Did Julia send you?" asks my Reece. He has his hands in his pockets.

"He looks like you, Daddy," says Mia.

"Let's get out of the cold. He doesn't have a jacket," I say.

We walk inside, and everyone takes a seat in the living room except for Mia. I have to pee and run to the restroom. When I return, the Reeces are looking at each other like they're watching a freak show. It's chilly, and I turn up the heat.

"How long were you in Dogtown?" I say. "You look great, by the way, considering the circumstances."

"I have no idea how long. It could have been years or just days. There's no way to gauge the passing of time. I hate to ask, but do you have some food I could eat? And a Coke or something?"

"I'll make you a bologna sandwich for now. I'm going to bake some salmon and make some rice for dinner." I rush to the kitchen and make the sandwich, slathering it with plenty of mayonnaise. It's unbelievable that the Reece I worked with is here. I asked Julia, and she delivered. I bring the sandwich to Reece with a can of Sprite. I want to watch him eat, but return to the kitchen and put the salmon in the oven with a dill and butter sauce, and put the rice on for twenty minutes.

"Were there other people in Dogtown with you?" I say.

"At first, there were, but they all magically disappeared. I was truly alone in that vast empty space, or so I thought. There could be others. Before I was whisked here, a little girl with bright golden hair appeared and said she was sending me home. She said her name was Julia. I felt like I was in the presence of a God and then, wham, I'm on your front porch."

He's out of the loop as he takes big bites, and I explain to him the situation with Dahlia and Julia. He takes it in, saying it's hard to believe, and he just wants to go home.

"Do you remember me from Gwar?" asks my Reece. "Things happened pretty fast at the end."

"Yeah, I was dumbfounded, and then those crazy little girls with knives came marching in. There were gunshots and then bright flashes of light, and then I was face down in what I learned was called Dogtown. There were groups of people standing around, all wanting to escape and find their daughters."

We explain the current situation with Dahlia and Julia,

that the world is in turmoil over who to follow, but that we believe in the goodness of Julia.

"That's so crazy," he says. "It's hard to believe." He's wearing jeans and a plain gray t-shirt. "Are you guys together? It seems you live together."

"We're married, about a year," says my Reece.

"I see," he says. "What do I do next? I'm so confused."

"You can stay here, right, Reece?" I say. "We have a third bedroom. Mia lives here with us, but it's a big house."

My Reece coughs. "We should call Markush and ask him about it. Plus, I need to call Kristin. In fact, I'll do that now." He explains who Markush is.

Reece gets Markush on the phone and tells him the story. It sounds like Markush is thrilled, and he tells Reece to bring him to Organon and the guest facility. We decide that Reece should spend the night with us and then head to Organon in the morning. I can't help but wonder if the other Emma will take note of this new Reece, who is her age and mine as well.

MULDRAUGH

I sleep late, till ten. Mia wakes us up, wanting breakfast. Reece lingers awhile, and I wash up and head to the kitchen downstairs. The new Reece is sitting in the stuffed chair, watching TV with the sound muted. His hair reaches his shoulders, having not been cut in Ethiopia for several months.

"Get up early? Sleep well?" I say. I'm wearing my striped pajamas with house shoes.

"Slept well but woke up early, just trying to fathom where I am. It was 1987 back in our universe, and here it's 1998. Everything looks the same, although I've noticed that you have hot water. In our world, hot water is unhealthy."

"Yeah, the hot water is strange, I admit, but I've gotten used to it. It actually feels good."

"How do you wake up with a hot shower?"

"You just do. You should try it. Want breakfast?"

"Sure."

I leave him for the kitchen and put on some water to boil for oatmeal, and then make some buttered toast. When it's ready, I yell upstairs that soup's on. The new Reece doesn't waste time and is the first to sit at the table. Mia joins us, and then my Reece stumbles through the living room.

"What are we doing today?" asks Mia. It's a teacher workday at her school, and she's home.

Reece rubs his eyes. He takes about an hour to wake up. "I don't know. Maybe show Reece the sights? There aren't many things to see in Muldraugh, though."

"I'm up for whatever you guys want to do," says the new

Reece. He's wearing a pair of Reece's corduroys and his zigzag sweater.

"We can show him around and then take him to Organon. I know that Markush wants him there, but he can stay here, I think." I watch Reece for a reaction.

"I guess, let Reece decide," my Reece says.

"Wherever is fine, but it would be nice to be close to you, to you guys," he says.

"We'll see," says my Reece. I can tell he is annoyed.

"Oh," I say, "how did the phone call with Kristin go last night?"

Reece explains that she wouldn't answer at first. She told him that he was in danger of being subjected to the wrath of Dahlia, that he was blaspheming Dahlia's name by commiserating with Julia. Reece learned that Kristin has been declared the mother of God, and she is taking her role very seriously. She kept bringing up Simon Klinefelter, referring to him as the Prophet. She did not ask about Mia. We all agree that she's gone to the dark side.

"Hey, let me smoke a cigar before we go? Reece, want a cigar?" asks my Reece.

"Sure, I love cigars."

They head out to the front porch in the chilly air and light up. Reece takes his cigars seriously, starting each day with one. I don't mind, but I hate the smell, like a burning tire.

"We'll do something fun in about an hour," I say to Mia. "Have any homework you need to do before we go?"

"Just reading a book. I need to read it again so I can do good on the test."

"What's the book?"

"It's an old *Happy Hollisters* book. The family has adventures together."

"Are you still reading *Pippi Longstocking?*"

"I finished that. I told Dad that I wanted to read *The Hobbit*. He's gonna buy it for me."

We chat, then head to the kitchen to do the dishes. Mia is polite, reserved like her dad, and very smart. I hear noise in the living room.

"Emma!"

Mia and I go to the living room. The Reeces are standing, looking at the TV with the volume raised.

"What's up?" I look at the TV, which is showing a crowd scene of protesters.

"There's been a shooting in Las Vegas. Someone opened fire on a group of demonstrators supporting Dahlia. Nine people are dead."

"Holy cow," I say.

The clip of the shooting plays. A street scene, and then there are loud pops and people scattering, many falling to the ground. We all take a seat and watch the Las Vegas incident.

"The first murders in over a year," says my Reece.

"Julia has lost it," I say. "This could be bad, is bad."

My Reece goes into detail about the conflict between Dahlia and Julia for the new Reece's benefit. The new Reece is having trouble understanding, and my Reece explains the role of Dahlia in abducting girls and parents, and then their return by Julia.

The video shifts to a news desk. Nine are dead and some twenty are injured. They go to a live feed from the Truth

Ranch in California. It's Klinefelter, wearing a red robe with a belt of white flowers. His big belly makes him seem pregnant. He stands in front of a group of microphones. Kristin is standing just behind him, looking tired but defiant. There's no sign of Dahlia. He first informs the world that Dahlia and her blessed mother, Kristin, have arrived at the ranch, then speaks of the Las Vegas murders.

"We condemn the shooting of our innocent members," says Klinefelter, "who were marching peacefully. Julia has shown her true colors and will destroy the universe as we know it. But with Dahlia by our side, we will reign victorious."

After an hour of watching the news and learning of militia groups taking sides in the ongoing conflict, we decide to show the new Reece the pride of Muldraugh, the Ritz diner, even though we're not really hungry. Mia gives some pushback, but she comes along.

We arrive at the diner, and there's something afoot. A large white banner with red lettering hangs across the front bank of windows. It reads, "Dahlia Go Home." We're somewhat shocked, but take our seats as usual, the floor nice and sticky. I recognize the waitress, Donna, as she whips out her little notepad. She looks like she's been sixty for years, with a boy's haircut. She's also wearing a Julia-is-Love t-shirt.

"What y'all have? Hi, little girl," says Donna. Mia says hi.

The Reeces get the special, chicken-fried steak with oven fries and a side of cabbage. I have the cheeseburger plate, and Mia gets the grilled cheese. The place is quieter than usual, not as busy.

"What about that sign? Is that new?" asks new Reece. His hairline is already receding at twenty-three, but not as bad as my Reece's.

"New to me," says my Reece. "That shooting will galvanize opinion, I'm sure."

"Yeah," I say, "Julia has let the murders happen. I'm surprised. Maybe she can't be everywhere at once."

"I think," says my Reece, "that Julia is modifying her attitude. She gets weary of Dahlia's influence. For some reason, she can't make her disappear."

We talk, and our orders arrive. The chicken-fried steak is hanging off the plates. Donna slaps the bill down on the table and waddles away.

"I hope that Julia doesn't become another Dahlia," I say.

"Then we'd be back to square one," says my Reece. "Things are getting scary."

A black pickup truck whirls into the parking lot, slinging gravel. We have a front-row seat as three men, with ballcaps and wearing camo, jump out and attack the cords holding up the sign. I can see their grim faces painted with purpose.

"What's going on?" asks Mia.

Everyone in the diner is looking and commenting. The men are just a few feet away on the other side of the glass. I notice that the manager is on the phone, but he's not stepping outside. The men jump back in the truck and peel off. I'm pretty sure that gravel hits my car.

"The hell," says new Reece.

"Wow," says my Reece. "It's getting very personal. I was afraid of this. Dahlia is still creating chaos and is at the root of this."

We pick at our food, and soon a police cruiser enters the parking lot. A lone cop wanders inside. It gets quiet again, everyone straining to hear what is being said. He speaks with the manager and takes notes. We decide to leave, Reece pays, and we head to Organon to introduce new Reece to Dr. Markush and to see the facility.

Inside, we sign in new Reece at the front desk. Markush is in his office, we learn, and we head that way down a long hall. His door is open.

"Hey, Doc!" says my Reece.

Markush is about to pick up the phone. He looks suave with his long, gray hair and two-day beard.

"Right on time," says Markush. "You must be Reece, the Reece from Gwar. You worked with Emma here." They shake hands, and we sit. "So, Reece, where have you been? Tell me."

"We were at the diner," says Mia, looking important.

"Ha," says Markush. "Right. But before you landed here, where were you?"

"Dogtown," says new Reece. "This endless white space without chairs, without anything. It happened when the others were transported back here, I think. It gets confusing."

"Ah, did you interact with anyone or with Julia?" asks Markush.

"Occasionally, I met small groups, but I could feel a tug toward something like a power source. In the distance, the light turned blue at some point, but I decided not to head that way. I had no idea what I might find. I think I was just caught up in some sort of vortex. But then, zap, and I'm here in Kentucky. I'm worried about my people back home."

Markush has lit up like a Christmas tree, even though he's Jewish. "I think you're right. You got lost in the shuffle. Somehow, Julia figured out the mistake and sent you here. But why did she send you here? Why not back to the clinic in Ethiopia or to your home?"

I don't know why I'm about to say this. "I have to confess that I spoke with Julia about him, asked her to look out for him, and take care of him." My neck is a little red with guilt.

"Hmm, that's interesting," says my Reece. "Did you ask her to bring him here? You must have."

I'm deep in it now. "I think I just said bring him home, and she took that as here. Just another minor slip-up. At least he's out of Dogtown."

New Reece speaks. "Whatever the reason, I'm just happy to be here, but it would be great if I could go home. What are the chances?"

I'm glad that he's speaking, taking the pressure off me. "Yeah, now we have three Reeces, plenty to go around." I try to laugh, but everyone is dead serious.

"Three Reeces," says Mia. "But just one dad, right. My daddy." She looks at my Reece like he's the king of the world.

"That's right, babydoll, one dad and one daughter." There should be a hug, but the moment passes.

Markush seems to reset, becoming serious. "I'm really worried about Kristin and Dahlia." His voice catches, and he sighs.

"She looked so pale and thin," says my Reece. "I would have never thought she would take off like that."

"I miss Mommy," says Mia. "She likes Dahlia better than me." She swings her legs in the big chair.

"Mommy loves you," says my Reece. "But she's being tricked by Dahlia. Mommy will come back."

"I'm so sorry she left," I say.

"Yeah, me too," says Markush. "I miss her. The house seems so empty. Dahlia was always creating havoc, and Kristin would scold her, but then she started letting Dahlia have her way. She's become more of an accessory than a mother."

"She's the mother of God, according to that Klinefelter character," says my Reece. "He's behind this for sure."

We talk more, commiserating with Markush and his loss of Kristin. He says he's on an antidepressant for the second time in his life, the first being after the death of his wife. Nationally, the group leading the charge for Julia is made up of people who organized JuliaCon. Markush says they have an extensive network nationwide with support from the Pentagon. Jim Tart is the spokesman for the group and gave an interview after the shooting, expressing dismay at the murders and saying that Julia was not responsible. He is clever and turned the situation around, directing the blame at Dahlia and her followers, accusing them of setting up the incident to attract more followers through sympathy. None of us is sure that could be the case, but these days, one never knows what the real truth is.

MULDRAUGH

The new Reece is staying in the guest facility at Organon per Markush's request. He wants to run the full battery of tests, including the head X-ray and possible mesh biopsy. I hope that after the tests are done, he can come live with us. We have so much to talk about. My Reece has been texting with the Alabama Emma against my wishes. We had a big argument last night about her and went to bed mad at each other. Mia was upset, and that makes me feel bad. She needs stability for sure. The other Reece and Emma are coming over for dinner.

 Reece and I worked our half-day shift at Organon, where I had the chance to talk with the new Reece. We reminisced about some of the patients at the clinic in Ethiopia, talking about trachoma and tapeworms. There is a definite spark between us that is lingering from our time together. Reece and I have been watching the news this afternoon, and I can't believe the chaos. The Las Vegas shooting has sparked demonstrations with acts of violence. The largest clash was in San Francisco, where Julia is favored. Up to four hundred people took to the streets. There were no shootings, but dozens were arrested or taken to hospitals. Those primarily injured were followers of Dahlia. We've heard there will be a Dahlia event in nearby Radcliff, and Reece and I want to see what happens, although Markush has warned us to stay out of the spotlight. At three, Reece goes to pick up Mia from school. She rushes in and asks if Kristin is okay, hearing news of the violence from Reece.

"She is fine. Homework before TV," I say to her. "Need any help?"

"No, just vocabulary words, and I'm reading *The Hobbit*. Ms. Turner said I wasn't old enough to read it, but I like it. I'm going to do a book report on it." She's taken up Reece's habit of working outside on the back porch, and she heads that way with a juice box.

Reece busies himself changing two lightbulbs, and I clean up the kitchen. There's a knock at the door, and the other Reece and Emma let themselves in. I notice right away they look so happy.

"Hey, guys!" I say. "You're early!"

"Hello, hello!" says the other Reece. He rushes to turn on the TV. "Big news from California."

My Reece comes in from out back. "What's up, brother?"

"Just watch," says the other Reece.

There's a scene of destruction, like a massive bomb went off. It's the front gate of The Truth Ranch where Kristin and Dahlia are. We listen in silence, the reporter saying that a car bomb went off. Apparently, a black van tried to ram the gate and exploded prematurely, killing the driver and shattering the gate. The blast blew out windows in buildings facing the explosion over a hundred feet away. A group called Julia Now! has taken responsibility and is being linked with JuliaCon.

"Unbelievable," says my Reece. "I hope Kristin is okay, and Dahlia too. This is insane."

The footage reverts to Simon Klinefelter. "By the grace of Dahlia and her blessed Mother, we will have revenge. Julia, if she exists, is cruel and violent. Today's events have proven that. We plan to have Dahlia address the world tomorrow morning." He makes a prayer gesture with his hands. "This is just the beginning of the end."

"He's slimy," says the other Reece. "Maybe he's getting what he deserves."

"I can't believe Julia is letting this happen," says the other Emma. She is sitting on her Reece's lap and kisses him.

We switch channels and get the news again. Half an hour passes, and I suggest that we go ahead and order pizza. Mia loves pizza, and I'm tired of cooking anyway. The pizza arrives, and Mia comes in from outside, her cheeks rosy.

"Where's the ham and onion pizza?" asks my Reece. I don't like the accusatory tone in his voice.

"Nobody likes that but you," I say.

"So, I don't matter?" he says.

"Hey, settle down," says the other Reece. "It's just pizza."

I can't help myself. "Reece has been texting the Emma in Alabama. He's obsessed with her." My bile is rising. I think I sound childish, but it's a blazing issue.

They take in the information but have no solution other than it's okay to talk with a friend. Hell, she saved his life. They worked hard in the clinic side by side in a foreign country under harsh conditions. I know that bond because I have it with the Reece I worked with. I cool down for the sake of Mia, but am by no means finished with the issue.

"Okay. So, we've aired our dirty laundry. Let's eat," says my Reece.

I agree, but notice that the other Emma and Reece are

uncomfortable, exchanging glances. It takes half an hour for the pizza to arrive. We eat in the living room in relative silence as "Wheel of Fortune" spins round on the TV. I notice a piece of spinach on Reece's teeth, and it irritates me. I'm still worked up and just want peace and for Reece to stop communicating with Emma.

"So, it's okay for you to drool over the new Reece?" asks my Reece. "You worked with him and can't wait to get your hands on him."

I'm in a quandary, knowing what he says is true. But we're married and things aren't looking good. "I'm not drooling, for God's sake, for Julia's sake. We just have a strong bond."

My Reece slumps in the overstuffed chair. "But that's the same thing I've been saying about Emma, Alabama Emma. I admit it. What's good for the goose is good for the gander."

"Guys, settle down," says the other Emma.

"How am I supposed to settle down when Reece is gaga over that Emma? I need a minute." This can't go on like this. Something must give. I walk to the kitchen and take a deep breath, scanning blankly inside the fridge. The other Emma joins me. "Why can't Reece and I be like you and Reece, happy and all lovey-dovey? I'm dying just to go home and cry with my mom."

"I get it. You're feeling betrayed, but I think your Reece is feeling the same way. Are you in love with the other Reece? Is he on board?" she says.

"I don't know. The urge to be with him is very strong. Earlier today, we talked in the lounge of the guest facility. I feel like we could talk forever about the clinic and the people in Ethiopia."

"Were you guys intimate?" she says.

"Not really, but we did kiss one night inside my house, and I was ready to go all the way, but I think he was scared to start something, being engaged. I guess technically he's still engaged, but he's in another universe now, so maybe it doesn't count. I just wish I had waited to get married. It seemed so perfect, though. We shared similar experiences in the clinic, but we didn't work together or suffer together. Ethiopia blew my mind, sister."

"Yeah, my mind is blown as well. Reece was your rock in the clinic, and you were his. You guys are going to have to make some hard decisions."

"Y'all coming back!" my Reece yells from the living room.

Emma and I return, looking guilty, no doubt. I glance at the TV and guess the puzzle: "Jack and Jill went up the hill." But then they came tumbling down.

"You guys okay?" asks the other Reece.

"Yeah, fine," I say.

We get off the topic of twisted love, and my Reece reminds us of a TV special that the Returnees have been invited to. Sherri Loveless is arranging the details. I wish that the new Reece could be there.

NEW YORK CITY

It seems warmer here in the city than in Fort Knox. We've arrived for our "tell all," fresh off a private jet from Fort Knox. Security is tight, and we have two MPs with rifles traveling with us. It's strange not having Kristin or Dahlia around. Everyone takes room service for dinner, and I'm exhausted. Reece and I didn't sit next to each other on the plane, raising eyebrows. We have been cross with each other, always about the other Reece and Emma. More and more, Reece strikes me as an old man set in his ways.

Around nine in the hotel restaurant, we all gather for a buffet breakfast. The ceilings are really high, and there are classical paintings hanging on the mauve walls. With scrambled eggs, sausage, bacon, and pineapple on my plate, I save a seat for Reece next to me, but he sits as far away as possible at a long table. I get the feeling that the others are talking about us, and it makes me sick. I thought Reece was the one, never imagining that the other Reece would magically appear.

"What a delightful feast," says Arthur. He wears the large napkin like a bib. Freshly showered, his white, graying hair is still wet. He especially likes the pancakes, but just with whipped cream. I notice the MPs, one male and one female, sitting together, and wave.

"Eat up because we may miss lunch," says Reece. "The taping starts at eleven." He's dressed neatly in black jeans and a loose black pullover. He looks like he should be at a funeral.

Afewerki's plate is filled only with fruit. "I am needing

these fruits. The food in the school cafeteria is without fruit sometimes." Reece agrees, having taught at the university for two years before his crisis with Dahlia and Mia.

"So, should we practice answering questions?" I say. I'm wearing a dress that now seems too formal.

"How will we know what questions will be asked?" asks Arthur. "I'm sure there will be inquiries into Dahlia and Julia."

"Let's just play it by ear and be natural," says Reece.

I prefer more structure, but I agree it is what we usually do. At ten, having rushed upstairs to brush my teeth with Reece, we take a van driven by one of the MPs. We're told he has crazy driving skills in case we are followed or ambushed. The drive is dizzying through tunnels and across a large bridge, which one I'm not sure. New York City is exciting, but I would hate to live here. It's just so big, and the traffic is from hell. We arrive at NBC studios in Rockefeller Plaza, and are let out and followed by the MP, who looks like a warrior with his uniform and rifle. There are perhaps a dozen people with signs. It looks like a gathering of Julia's followers. There is noise above the din, and a lone man with long black hair is chastising the demonstrators. The MP leads us around the group and into a three-story building with a "Today Show" banner, wrapping two sides. I had expected we would be mobbed, but no one seems to recognize us or does not care.

Inside the green room, we are dusted with makeup and have our hair situated. Arthur is taken with the young lady attending to him and allows her to apply hairspray. Afewerki seems uncomfortable and is very quiet today. He wants to wear his Exxon ballcap, but was advised not to.

Emma

"What a hell," he says.

At ten to one, a bubbly young lady leads us down a hallway and to the TV set. One side is a jumble of cameras and equipment, and the other looks like someone's living room, fitted with five lemon-colored chairs. We're introduced to the moderator, Matt Kuger. He is friendly but all business. He is tall, thin, and has copper hair, which is unusual. His midwestern accent and cool demeanor make him a regular kind of guy, which I like. At one o'clock, we're seated and given instructions not to curse, if possible, to be natural. They do not want us to incite violence and caution us to be as objective as possible. I'm nervous, of course, and am glad that I'm seated beside Reece. "Truce for now?" asks Reece, and I agree with a smile.

Facing the cameras, we sit in a semicircle with Matt facing our middle. He keeps looking at a card, fishing for it from his coat pocket. They do a countdown, and a serious smile pops onto Matt's face. He introduces himself, and then each of us shares some background on Dahlia and Julia before he begins to ask questions.

"We're all still shocked by the shooting in Las Vegas. Who do you think was responsible?" he says.

Reece speaks. "Well, the shooter is responsible, but I get your question. The shooter was terribly sorry and seems to have been under a spell of some sort. I think that Julia allowed it to happen, though. She sprinkled fairy dust at first and brought peace, but she's making an exception with Dahlia."

"Reece, your ex-wife Kristin took Dahlia to California to live at The Truth Ranch, where there was a car bombing last week. Is Julia jealous that Dahlia has a mother?"

"I don't know. Dahlia kept Julia captive for an eternity, and I think Julia resents that and is seeking to neutralize her. I don't think she can destroy Dahlia, but a Dahlia in human form can suffer."

"And the latest development," says Matt, "is the appearance of another Reece who I believe worked with Emma in a clinic in Ethiopia. Tell us about him."

It's my turn to speak, but I worry that my words will not meet the moment. "Yeah, we worked together in a village called Gwar, which is on another planet, possibly in another universe. We clicked and ran the clinic together. I would have gone nuts if he had not been there."

"Yes," says Arthur, "he is a younger version of the Reece we have with us today. He longs for his home much as I do my own."

"I wonder why he was placed here?" asks Matt.

"Emma here prayed to Julia for his return, and she sent him here, much to Emma's delight." Reece reaches over and touches my thigh, and I push his hand away.

"Emma, why did you call back this other Reece, if that is the right language?" asks Matt. I can tell he is really into this, so I need to answer truthfully while choosing my words carefully.

"I was worried about his safety. We were very close. When we were returned, Dahlia had unleashed a small army of little girls with knives. Reece, the one from Gwar, was caught up in the return but was 'accidentally' sent to Dogtown. He was just lost in the shuffle, but I'm glad that he's safe and sound."

"So, is Julia God? She seems to have some imperfections, like jealousy. Afewerki, what do you think?"

Afewerki is the shyest among us, and I feel for him. He rubs his head and, looking down, speaks. "Julia cannot be God. God is not a little girl." He is sincere in his beliefs, despite being transported to this planet and witnessing the power of Julia.

"What do others think?" asks Matt.

"I do not believe in a God, per se," says Arthur, "but Julia exhibits the greatest power I have ever known. I never thought I would be tempted to acknowledge a higher power, but Julia certainly meets the criteria. I have come to know her as a kind and understanding being who has our best interests at heart. Why she has allowed violence recently, I do not understand."

The show is scheduled to be an hour-long special, but I soon learn that our session will last some five hours. Every hour or so, we take a break.

"Where do we go from here?" asks Matt, asking the last question.

I have an answer. "I think we have to acknowledge Julia as the primary God for now and see Dahlia as a special human with special powers. Many will choose Dahlia as the model we have been used to for ages. In that model, humans are basically evil but capable of good works. I apologize to Afewerki, but you have seen her abilities." I notice him mumble.

Reece and Arthur put their two cents in, basically agreeing with me, and the interview is over. We then take an hour doing still shots, and then we are done. I wanted to mention the relationship of my Reece with the Alabama Emma. Maybe the media haven't got wind of that yet. I'm exhausted and looking forward to our dinner at an

Italian restaurant.

The restaurant, Clio's, is walking distance from our hotel on Grand Street. It's not Little Italy, but more in Lower Manhattan, from what I understand. The MPs follow behind us as we navigate the crowded sidewalks. I make a move and grab Reece's hand, which he takes. I'm a mess inside, thinking about the new Reece, but I need to focus on the moment and make the best of it.

A green awning covers Clio's entrance. The doors are tall and have brass poles that you pull on, but a man in a red velvet coat opens and holds the door for us. Seeing the fancy inside, I'm just glad that we have Organon credit cards.

We make the MPs sit with us at a table for six. They look uneasy as they lean their rifles against the table. Ornate paintings cover the walls, and there are little nooks with marble statues of what seem to be nymphs. We have been sitting for about five minutes, and no server has come to take our orders. Arthur is grumpy and hungry and complains. A man with a mustache approaches our table. He looks like the manager, bald and short.

"Sir, we are in need of attendance as we are famished," says Arthur.

The man scowls and has trouble speaking, as if he were about to explode.

"You, you must leave immediately. I recognize you, and you are not welcome here!" He gestures with his hands. His nametag says Frank.

Reece stands. "What the hell are you talking about? We need food."

Frank looks frightened but does not back down. Everyone is staring, and someone shouts, "Long Live Julia!" That really sets Frank off, and he makes an announcement that all followers of Julia must leave.

There is an uproar, and people are shouting. The MPs go into attack mode and shield us with rifles ready. Frank gets into a shoving match with a tall man wearing a brown beret. Frank slaps the beret, and the guy swings back, hitting Frank square between the eyes. I'm floored and have trouble taking it all in.

"What a hell," says Afewerki right on cue. He and the rest of us weave through the melee toward the entrance with the MPs right behind us. Arthur catches a cuff on his temple and curses. Outside, underneath the awning, we gather our wits. Several more diners exit amid shouting from inside. I hold onto Reece.

"Damn, that was rude," says Reece. He reminds me of a cat that has been ruffled.

"I can't believe it," I say. "This is ridiculous."

"We are being persecuted for our beliefs by scoundrels of Dahlia," says Arthur.

"We must go some place new to eat," says Afewerki. "I do not like this."

Regrouped, the MPs advise us to do room service, but Reece is determined to eat out. I've lost my appetite, but follow along. We find a bar/bistro two blocks away and enter, feeling like we're being watched, and we are. It's dim inside with a bar to the right and a few tables to the left. A pool table lingers in the back. I notice a small portrait labeled Julia on a shelf behind the bar. The bartender tells us to take any table, and we join two tables. This time, one

MP stands guard inside and one outside. Reece's phone rings, and it's the other Reece. He and the other Emma are watching Mia while we're gone.

"That was Reece," he says. "Dahlia made an appearance at their house and took Mia's favorite stuffed bunny."

"What?" I say. "Good Lord, what's next?"

"Damn, I truly do hate that little girl. She abducted Mia twice, put her in a cage at a circus."

"I can attest to that," says Arthur.

Our waitress arrives with small glasses of water and takes our orders. It's all bar food: shepherd's pie, beef stew, fish and chips. We order draft beers, even Afewerki, who usually does not drink.

"I guess the war is on," says Reece. "I hope Dahlia doesn't make a habit of terrorizing Mia or us, for that matter. We just need to get back."

Our flight leaves at ten tomorrow, so we can't jet back right away. We review the day, and my Reece gets stuck on the new Reece, saying that he might be an agent of Dahlia. I've noticed that he has been increasingly paranoid over the last few weeks. He's bipolar and takes meds, but I never see him taking the pills, and that worries me. He leans into me and whispers.

"That guy against the brick wall has Dahlia written all over him." I watch Reece stare at him.

"That's ridiculous," I say. "How can you tell?"

"It's in his eyes," says Reece. "I've a good mind to wear him out." He clenches his fists and leans forward as if he is about to attack.

"No, Reece. Stay put, man," I say.

Arthur and Afewerki look at the accused man and exchange glances. He takes notice and gives us a what-the-hell look.

"Goddamn spies everywhere," says Reece. I rub his back to calm him down.

MULDRAUGH

Reece and I work our day shift at Organon, then head home. There's a new patient who had been comatose for seven years before Julia released him from Dogtown. He can't walk yet and is as weak as a noodle. He has the mesh, and a biopsy is scheduled. We've decompressed over our TV special, but Reece is so focused on the new Reece. I spoke with the new Reece for about half an hour this morning. He's bored and wants to get out and about, so I've invited him over for dinner, and Reece is not happy. I pick up Mia at three from school and head home.

"Did you finish *The Hobbit?*" I say.

"Yeah. It was great. I just love Bilbo and even Gollum. I want to read *The Lord of the Rings* next."

The day is slack and lazy with fluffy white clouds. I've noticed that the winds have picked up, perfect to fly a kite.

"We'll get that for you asap," I say. "You're so smart and such a great reader."

"Thanks," she says.

At home, Reece is raking dead leaves. He wants to burn the leaves in a big pile, but we can't have a fire in the city limits. He flat-out argued with me about it, but finally gave in.

"Hey, farmer!" I say.

"Daddy!" says Mia.

"Hey, baby!" says Reece, and she runs to him and takes the rake.

"I learned a new word today, bumptious. It means you're a sourpuss. I love new words," says Mia, and she lets the rake fall to the ground.

"Done already?" asks Reece. "I guess you want to go read a book."

"I have some homework first. Mommy said you would buy me *The Lord of the Rings*."

"Oh, wow, big-person books," says Reece.

Mia runs into the house, most likely to get a snack first. I follow and wonder what to do next. I need to vacuum, but don't have it in me today. Reece comes inside with a strange look, holding his cell phone.

"What's up?" I say.

"Just talked with Markush. There's been a development."

"What? Tell me."

"You know that lady who helped me and Arthur find Mia? Caroline Marquette?"

"Yeah, what about her?"

"She's here. She popped into Organon an hour ago. Markush figured out who she was pretty quickly."

I think about my prayers to Julia to bring the lady here for Arthur. "Wow! What do we do with her?"

"She's going to stay in the guest facility, not the guest house. Markush wants to surprise Arthur and wants us to be there."

It's about three-thirty, and the new Reece is coming for dinner at six. We can go on base, meet Caroline, and bring Reece to the house, I suggest. Reece is instantly defensive and gets ugly with me. Of course, I remind him about his infatuation with Alabama Emma. He plays it off, and we jump in the car. Mia is fine to stay by herself.

We park and walk inside Organon, greeting Denise.

Markush is in the nursing station on the medical unit, scribbling in charts. We let him finish up, and he gives us the plan. Reece leaves to fetch Arthur, and they arrive within ten minutes.

"What is this excitement about?" asks Arthur. He's wearing his baggy black trousers and a button-up shirt with ruffles down the middle.

"Get ready to have your mind blown," says Reece.

"I fear that sounds painful," says Arthur.

We check into the guest facility, and there she is, sitting on a couch, sipping a cup of cranberry juice. She turns to look, and I swear her jaw hits the ground.

"Herr Schopenhauer!" she says, standing with a bewildered look. She's wearing a long, old-fashioned, green dress that is nicely pleated at the bottom. She has a fine figure and tousled, long, dark hair. "How do I find you here, you bag of bones?"

"My god!" says Arthur. "It's Caroline." His ruddy face softens as he approaches and takes her hand. "Caroline, my dear, where have you come from?"

Caroline says, "From a terrible place, a rustic village where women fetch the water, walking an hour and a half. I had to eat, so I was engaged as a water carrier. The pots were immense and heavy as lead. An ox kicked a young boy and sent him flying to the moon. I'm so glad to be gone from there, but I fear I am no closer to home."

Markush beams. "You guys sit and chat. I have some business to attend to."

There are two hard couches facing one another, and we sit, followed by an awkward silence.

"Why did you leave me so alone?" asks Caroline.

Emma

"I didn't leave you; you left me, if you remember. You wore the Abba's vest and called upon Dahlia. You disappeared, my love. If I may, I am quite glad to see you." Arthur stands, stoops, and kisses her hand, which she extends for him. They certainly make a cute couple, although Arthur is much older.

"And Reece, I thought I would never see you again. Did your search for your daughter prove fruitful?" asks Caroline.

"Yes, Mia is alive and well. She's at school. We found her as you were getting lost in the ether."

"Ether indeed," says Caroline. "More like fire and brimstone."

I'm looking around for the new Reece, who is staying here in the guest facility with Caroline. I want to ask if he's in his room or check myself, but I'm afraid that Reece will get mad. Arthur has seated himself next to Caroline, and they are having a blast, it seems. It's a long way from the story of Arthur pushing her down the stairs in Berlin, followed by a lawsuit. I feel like I've done something good, asking Julia to bring her here.

The other Reece and Emma join us for a few minutes and make Caroline's acquaintance. She's baffled by our mirror looks and doesn't seem to understand. She is quite peppy, and I learn that she's a seamstress. I feel a sense of relief from her as she adjusts to the new place. We laugh when she asks about the lights and the TV, and try our best to explain in simple terms. Reece says we'll take her to the world-famous Ritz diner sometime this week, his go-to for introducing people to the area.

Reece and I take our leave after an hour. It turns out

that the new Reece is walking around the lake and will be back in a few minutes, so we wait for him. I have butterflies in my chest.

We wait for him outside on a bench, and he pops into the parking lot from the road. He waves. I wave.

"Hey, buddy!" I say and give him a side hug. My Reece folds his arms across his chest.

"Hey, and hello!" He shakes my Reece's hand. "I'm ready to go. Brushed my teeth and everything."

My Reece drives, and I sit in the front. The car still smells new, which I like. I turn to talk with the new Reece, and it's like we're back in the clinic again. We talk about a very sick woman who presented with severe malnutrition and jaundice. She was on the verge of death. We hydrated her and put in a feeding tube, which we used to push liquid Nido. She didn't urinate for a day, but we kept pushing fluids, and she came out of her semi-comatose state and started peeing like a racehorse. My Reece says he and the new Emma had a very similar experience.

Mia greets us at the front door, having become scared when the mailman knocked. She didn't answer, and I wonder what the mailman was trying to deliver. The house smells of the pork roast in the crock pot, and I get busy making mashed potatoes and heating some sauerkraut, to which I add a half teaspoon of caraway seeds.

"Such a day," I say, joining them in the living room. *CNN* is on the tube with a story about a violent confrontation between supporters of Dahlia and Julia. We notice in a running headline at the bottom that there has been a new development at Organon with news to follow. How information gets out so fast is the doing of Markush and

Sherri Loveless, I'm sure.

My Reece tells new Reece about Caroline and her connection with the search for Mia. He says she's attractive but belligerent, which raises my eyebrows. I just want to be alone with this other Reece and talk and talk. My Reece takes over the conversation, discussing clinic work and the shelter for homeless women and children, which was a dirty mess in my village. Strangely, my Reece asks if new Reece has ever heard voices, and that Julia was listening at that very moment. That allows me to talk about Julia and the state of the world, which is getting more heated day by day. At the small church we go to, a group of teenagers toilet-papered the trees and left a large Dahlia sign in front. Every day, I find something new in the yard, like a bicycle tire or a broken plastic chair. Reece is convinced that we're being watched and tormented with the rubbish in the yard. I think it's a single person who has loose ends and try to talk Reece down, but he's persistent.

"They're going to do a biopsy of my brain, I think," says the new Reece. "Something about mesh."

Reece and I laugh and tell him that it's just the scalp and not the brain. Markush has kept us updated about research into the mesh. It contains some kind of thallium that stores information. At the lab, they've found a way to interface with the mesh and read the data, which is all numbers. The amount of data is staggering, says Markush.

Mia comes downstairs and asks if it's time to eat. I almost forget that we are eating and scurry to the kitchen and have Mia set the table. Dinner goes okay, helped by a bottle of wine.

"So, are you wanting to go home?" asks my Reece. "Like

Emma?" He's doodling the sauerkraut on his plate. "Maybe y'all would get together again." His eyes look a bit hollow.

The new Reece clears his throat and glances at me. "Of course, I would like to go home, but how?"

"Well, you could ask Julia. She seems to have her nose in everyone's business," says my Reece.

"There's the Abba Paulos, too," I say. "With the Ark of the Covenant." I tell him about his appearance in Denver. We met him briefly there, but he had insisted on returning home immediately, being out of his element.

"Hmm, the Abba and the Ark sound a bit dicey," says new Reece. "I'd be up for trying with Julia, though, as crazy as it sounds."

Mia finishes her plate and asks to be excused to read. I've ordered her the *Lord of the Rings* books on this new website called Amazon, which I just learned about. We soon finish, and all I have for dessert are banana Moon Pies, but we enjoy them. I load the dishwasher and then join the boys in the living room, where they stare at the TV. Buried by the constant news of Julia and Dahlia, the presidential election is in November. The current administration has been notably quiet, given the chaos, but supports Dahlia as being best for the country. The Republican candidate, Thomas Crinkle, is promising that both Dahlia and Julia will be put in their places so that the real God can bless the nation. He also wants to ban abortion and clear the country of illegal immigrants. Reece says that every time Crinkle opens his mouth, a dead baby falls out. We're putting our vote to the American Independent Party, which is all about Julia and liberty, and the candidate

Emma

has a decent chance with twenty percent of the vote thus far, according to polls.

To get away from the news, I suggest we watch *Seinfeld*. It's the episode where Jerry and George buy an ice cream truck for Kramer to drive. I'm not interested, and I wish I could talk with new Reece alone.

It's a week later. Caroline and new Reece have moved to the guest apartments. Arthur is still there, and Markush has moved back as well, so one apartment remains open. Caroline and Arthur are getting along famously, although Caroline is very demanding and somewhat cows Arthur, which is funny to watch. Clashes between Dahlia and Julia supporters continue to escalate. Markush is very worried about our safety, and so am I.

"I think we need cameras," says Reece. He's wearing a yellow, happy-face t-shirt, which makes his eyes look a little crazy.

"I agree." I'm thinking that Reece's paranoia is justified, but it makes him so anxious, and he takes everything so personally. He got up twice last night with the baseball bat and roamed the yard.

The doorbell rings, and Reece goes into combat mode, looking through the curtains. "Looks like the mailman," he says and opens the door quickly. They exchange a few words, and Reece signs for a certified letter.

"Who's it from?" I ask. I'm still in my polka-dot PJs, and Mia is at school.

Reece turns the letter over, holds it up to the light. "Could be a trick," he says. Without answering me, he opens the letter with a butter knife and unfolds three pages of handwriting. I try to look, and he turns away.

"You gonna tell me?" I say with hands on hips.

"Uh, it's from Emma. I need to read this alone."

"Emma? Why is she sending you letters?"

"I don't know." The letter is folded, so I can't read it. He goes to the kitchen with a sigh, and I follow.

"I need to know what's in that letter, Reece."

"Wait!"

His tone is angry, and I sit opposite as he stands in front of the refrigerator, reading slowly as if sipping sweet tea on a hot summer day.

"Reece?" He ignores me and reads for a full five minutes, finally folding the letter and placing it on the table.

I'm afraid to grab it. "Can I read it?"

"I don't think so. It's personal." He looks defiant.

"Does she want you?"

"Of course she wants me."

"And do you want her...over me?" I'm about ready to start crying.

"Oh hell, don't cry." He mellows just a bit, running his hand through his thin mahogany hair.

"Reece, we're married, and she wants to break us up. Can't you see?"

"She wants me to visit soon, and I will do that, this time alone."

"God almighty," I say. "If you do that, then we're done. You've had the hots for her ever since you worked with her." I can't help but cry.

Reece ignores me and stares at the wall. I want to call the other Emma, the one married to the other Reece, and see what she thinks.

"What about Reece, the young one you like so much? Every chance you get, you have him cornered, talking his ear off," he says.

"Don't change the subject!" I say. "Yeah, go on and visit with your precious Emma. I've had it. And you need to take your medicine. I haven't seen you take it for a month."

"I'm not my true self on meds," he says. "I've got this energy, and I need to keep it going. But now you're changing the subject."

"Your true self will kill you," I say. "You're up all night and paranoid as hell."

"I'm getting Mia from school, and then I'm headed to see Emma. I'll be back Sunday, if you're lucky."

Rupert is barking, and Reece pulls back the curtain and scans the yard. He runs to the back door and steps onto the back porch. I'm at my limit and watch TV. It's bad. States have been officially declaring support for Dahlia, Julia, and the former God Almighty. In twelve states, including Alabama and Wyoming, the National Guard has defected to Julia and joined with militia groups. Other states, such as Delaware and Maryland, have declared for Dahlia. In Racine, Wisconsin, there is a standoff between federal troops and the National Guard. The city has been virtually shut down. The presidential candidates are having a field day, proclaiming their allegiances and plans for the future. Thomas Crinkle, the Republican, is the most vocal and downright nasty, saying that he will crush Dahlia and Julia and return the real God to His place.

Reece calls and sets up a time for an alarm and camera system to be installed before he gets Mia. I don't believe that he will actually take off to see his Emma. But once he's back with Mia, he packs a small bag and, without saying anything, grabs the car keys.

"You're going?" I say. "Don't ignore me!"

"I'll be back Sunday," he says.

"That's two nights away," I say. "If you go, don't plan on coming back. Mia and I will be fine here by ourselves."

"Mia's coming with me."

"Oh, Mia needs yet another mom!" I'm pissed and feeling helpless. "It's not your car, for God's sake."

"It's our car, and I'm going."

"Fine! Go!"

Mia comes downstairs with a small, pink suitcase, looking afraid.

"Why are y'all fighting?" she says.

"Your dad is being a dick," I say.

"Watch it," he says. "Come on, let's go. We have a six-hour drive, and there will be roadblocks."

"Mia, if you need anything or get scared, you can call me, okay?" I write my phone number on the back of a wine label. "Put this in a safe place." She puts the paper in her pocket. I address Reece one last time. "Does Markush know you're doing this?"

"No, and he can go to hell. He's just using us for his own gain."

And out the door they go after Mia hugs me. I've become fond of Mia and would hate to lose her. Feeling helpless, I call the guest facility and ask to speak with the new Reece. It takes a minute, and then I hear his voice, which sounds just like my Reece's voice.

"Hey! It's Emma! How are you?" I feel silly saying that, as I had seen him in the morning and had a long chat.

"Hey! Which Emma?"

"I live in Muldraugh, that Emma."

"I was hoping it was you. What's up?"

I explain that Reece left with Mia to see the other

Emma in Alabama. My voice cracks, and he asks if I'm okay, suggesting I have dinner at Organon. I don't have a car, though, and think that Markush can come and take me. By the time I hang up, I'm in tears. I call Markush, and he can't pick me up but says that he'll have Denise, the receptionist, pick me up at five-thirty. That gives me plenty of time to shower and get ready.

Denise is right on time. She's a cutie with soft brown hair and brown eyes. We chat, and I inevitably tell her of my troubles with Reece. She's sympathetic but doesn't have any real advice other than to talk with Julia, which I had not thought of. I take a moment and whisper a prayer, asking for love to reign supreme.

At Organon, I walk down the hall, and it's freezing as usual. The guest facility is open, and I walk in, feeling sheepish.

"Hello, young lady!" says Caroline. "I do hope you'll stay awhile. It's so very dull in here."

"Hi, Caroline," I say. "Is Reece around?"

"Yes, you should examine his room, but then let's chat."

I walk down the short hallway and peer into rooms. Reece is in the last room on the left. "Hey, soldier!" I used to call him soldier back at the clinic.

He's folding a shirt and drops it onto the bed. "My friend!" he says. "You're looking good as usual.

"Thanks, and you too." I blush a little.

As if led by a string, we walk back to the common area and join Caroline on the couches.

"My, what a happy couple," says Caroline.

"I'm married to the other Reece," I say. "But thanks anyway."

Caroline complains about the tests she has been taking, saying they are cumbersome. She talks about her job as a seamstress in Berlin, and she misses her mother badly. I'm curious about her and Arthur, and ask.

"He's a cranky old man, but I have grown very fond of him, and he is likewise fond of me. He's coming to dine with me very soon."

"You guys worked together to help find Mia, with Reece. That must have been trying," I say.

Caroline lights up. "Yes, it was very difficult. The place was Gadam, an infernal town where all buildings looked alike. There was no food, just the liquid called buster, which did come in a variety of delicious flavors."

Just then, Arthur arrives from the guest house, wearing black jeans and a holiday sweater.

"Arthur! My dear!" says Caroline as she stands. She rushes Arthur and grabs his hands. "I thought you may have forgotten about poor me. My, don't you look snappy with that sweater, a very nice wool."

Arthur has trouble speaking. "Yes, well, very good to see you as well." Caroline won't let go of his hands, and I expect them to start dancing.

"Call me 'my sweet,'" says Caroline. "You must, since you pushed me down all those years ago."

"Yes, quite...and I did not push you. I merely nudged you, and then you lay upon the ground like a rabbit."

"Let's not quibble," says Caroline, and lets his hands go. "Join me here on the couch."

Reece and I take the other couch. I would like for him to call me 'my sweet,' as well.

"Emma, where is your husband?" asks Arthur. He sits

ramrod straight with his hands in his lap.

I explain to him that Reece took off for Alabama. I don't say we're basically done, but let everyone know how pissed I am.

"And I have met this other Reece? I'm confused as I should be," says Caroline. She is taking up more than her fair share of the couch, squeezing Arthur into the corner. Just the sight of them makes me want to laugh.

"Yes, you've met him. He's older than Reece here." I give Reece a little side pinch.

"Ouch, sister," he says as if disturbed from a great sleep. He tousles my hair, which feels good. My sex life with Reece, my husband, has been pretty slim lately due to his paranoia, I think.

"Are you sure you are not betrothed to one another? You seem very much like a couple to me," says Caroline.

Arthur growls. "She is, I daresay, married to the other Reece. But with Julia, there is only love between us all."

Caroline has questions about Julia and Dahlia, and we answer as best we can. I say that something dreadful is coming down the pike and that we must be ready. Markush has warned us, and Reece is expecting the worst.

"Is there no peace under heaven?" asks Caroline. "I fully expect Arthur to protect me at all times, I do. Is that clear, Arthur, my dear?" She pats his leg, and he puts his hand on top of hers.

"To the best of my ability, pussycat." He rolls his eyes, and I laugh. They're about as entertaining as Laurel and Hardy.

"Pussycat," says Reece. "That's royal."

"Arthur, now be kind and sweet. I am far from home,

and you are my only connection with that place, which I love dearly," says Caroline.

"Yes, my pet. Together as one." Arthur appears uneasy, bobbing his knee up and down.

Dinner arrives, and there are extra trays for Reece and me. I watch Caroline as she gazes at her tray. There is a look of wonder, a pinched face, as if perusing a magazine and finding a great recipe. She's endless entertainment. The meal consists of pulled pork, cole slaw, and fries with iced tea.

"There is ice in this drink," says Caroline. "The ice makes it much too cold." She takes a sip and frowns. I have never had cold tea before, a bit like biting an acorn."

"Yes, I have even seen coffee with ice in this place," says Arthur. "One must adapt and be thankful for what one has."

"I am so grateful that you are here," she says. "This meat is lovely. There is a sauce that is unfamiliar."

"Ha, that's barbecue sauce," says Reece.

"Quite overpowering," she says.

I've got a direct line of sight to the TV mounted on the wall. My mouth is full, and I point and then hurry over. "It's Kristin and Dahlia!" Reece and Arthur come quickly, but Caroline takes her time.

Kristin and Dahlia are sitting in matching chairs, and Kristin is speaking. Her eyes look as vacant as an old motel. She seems to be reading from cue cards. Dahlia slouches beside her with a wicked little grin. Kristin says that since the car bomb attack, the forces of Dahlia have rallied, and that no resistance should be given to recognizing her as God. She goes on about being the divine mother and nurturing Dahlia. We listen in amazement and have to explain to Caroline who Kristin is and repeat our stories about Dahlia. The segment continues for another five minutes before returning to the news desk, where updates are provided on the various protests and stand-offs occurring around the country and the world. I learn there is to be a huge demonstration at the Capitol in a couple of weeks, organized by JuliaCon, and that violence is predicted. The face of JuliaCon is Jim Tart, a bubbly man with thick, short, black hair that seems fake. The president is calling for calm, which he does every day, it seems.

Crime is still rare, except for confrontations between supporters of Julia and Dahlia, and no one under one hundred is dying, which still seems crazy. Julia is definitely in the power seat, with her eyes on Dahlia. Interesting events are happening around the world. The government of Nigeria has declared Julianism the official religion. As here, followers of Julia are allying with followers of traditional gods. Hundreds of people there have died in conflicts between the camps, and the government has declared a state of emergency. It seems that Julia is willing to let her devotees perish when engaged in the cause.

"Such turmoil," says Caroline. "I fear this supersedes the romps of Napoleon."

"As his armies passed through the Confederation, I betook myself to a small town for safekeeping," says Arthur.

Their words remind me that they are from another world and have had full lives before coming to this world, just like me. A couple of hours have passed, and Caroline has been chatting up Arthur nonstop. I'm thinking I would like to be alone with Reece and keep checking my watch. Finally, Arthur makes a move.

"My lady, the hour grows late, and I must retire," he says.

"You don't enjoy my company?" she says, looking miffed.

Arthur frowns. "Yes, I value your company, but there is a phenomenon called sleep to which I aspire." He stands with difficulty and brushes his sleeves.

Caroline hops up and is ready for a parting embrace, but Arthur merely takes her hand and kisses it.

"When will I see you again?" she says, looking forlorn.

"Yes, tomorrow, perhaps. I will give you a tour of my abode if you like. It's quite nice. Well, I leave you with good wishes."

"Such a gentleman," she says. "I'm very fond of him, you know."

"One of the greatest thinkers of all time," says Reece. "Your Reece taught a class on his philosophy at the university, right?"

"Yep," I say. "He worships the old man."

Caroline is in no mood to call it a night, and I'm worried she'll never go to bed. She talks more about Gadam and then her life in Berlin. Finally, after another very long hour, she yawns and says that she will "take her leave and leave us young lovers to our desires." Both Reece and I laugh at that and wish her a good night.

"Jesus," I say, "she's a talker." There's an instant change of atmosphere, and it feels as if we are floating.

"So, Reece up and left to see Emma in Alabama? When's he coming back?" Reece puts his arm on the back of the couch behind me.

"He certainly did and took Mia with him. I guess he wants Mia to get used to her so that he can hook up with her. He said he's coming back on Sunday."

"We should do something tomorrow. We have the day off."

His hand drops onto my right shoulder, and I'm reliving our time together in Ethiopia. We had made it to the point of kissing, but nothing further. We go to silent mode, and thus it begins.

ORGANON

Well, I spent the night with Reece, and it's official. I'm in love, and so is he, I'm pretty sure. I get up early, make a spot on the couch with a blanket, and welcome Caroline as she strides into the common area. She looks suspicious, and I can tell that she knows.

"My, you slept on this hard couch," she says with a sly look.

"Uh, yep, on the couch. Not bad at all," I say.

"Yes, well, that is interesting, as there are other beds."

I laugh. "Ready for breakfast?" I say to change the subject.

"These breakfasts are meager, I'm afraid." She's wearing a long black dress that is tattered along the hem.

"You know, would you like to go shopping for clothes?" I say. "Your dress is a bit rough for the wear."

"Oh, that would be lovely," she says. "I've been wearing the same dress for months on end." She lowers her voice. "And some underthings as well."

The door opens, and an elderly woman pushes a cart with two breakfast trays. Just then, Reece appears in jeans and a t-shirt. The woman sees me and asks if I need breakfast. I say, "Sure thing," and thank her.

We gather at the dining table, and Caroline unveils her breakfast. "These eggs are much too firm, and what is this?" She points.

Reece laughs. "Those are grits made from corn."

"I see," she says and takes a bite. "Quite tasteless."

"You need some syrup to go on the grits," says Reece.

He's waiting to eat until my tray arrives, which it does.

We eat in silence. I can hear Caroline chewing her bacon.

"Let's go shopping on Monday, in the afternoon after my shift," I say to break the silence.

"What day is this? I'm so lost," says Caroline.

"Today is Saturday," says Reece.

We eat and talk about the weather, how it snows in winter, and is very hot in summer. I'm feeling very guilty about my trespasses with this Reece, but want to bring him home with me. It would be great for Reece to be there when my Reece returns tomorrow. I'm not sure what I would like to happen, but I have to follow my heart, and I'm sure that my Reece is cheating on me. Despite my bad behavior, I want to call and see what Reece has to say about his visit with Emma. I'm sure that they've misbehaved as well and feel very jealous.

Caroline agrees to go shopping on Monday. Maybe we'll get her something sexy and see how Arthur reacts. I can tell that he likes her, but is perhaps wary of the age difference. I broach the idea of Reece coming with me. I should ask Markush if it's okay, but he's out of town, and I don't want to bother him.

"Shall we?" I say to Reece. I'm hoping that Denise can take us home, and she agrees.

The drive home takes about ten minutes, and something is terribly wrong. Reece and I jump out of the car and see billowing smoke coming from the front porch. The house is on fire. My first thought is the cat and Rupert in the back.

"Shit, have to get the cat!" I say as I dial 911.

Emma

The front porch is an inferno, and we go through the fence to the back door, which is open. Rupert is barking but can get away from the house. I don't see the cat, and tell Reece to go upstairs while I look downstairs. A front window cracks with a bang, and flames leap onto the curtains. I check the kitchen again, opening cabinets, but there's no Tweezer. I hear Reece running down the stairs over the roar and crackle, and he's holding Tweezer. Within five minutes, the fire department arrives and begins to drown the flames.

The fire out, Denise leaves, and we talk with the fireman and a policeman. I'm sure it was arson, and they agree that it's a possibility, having found a melted gas container on the porch. After an hour, we get the all-clear and enter through the back door. The living room is a wreck from the smoke and water, but was spared. I put Tweezer for safekeeping in an upstairs bedroom.

"Holy cow," I say. "That was close." I'm shivering in the chill air.

"This has to be arson. Dahlia's gang, no doubt," says Reece. He's my hero for saving the cat.

"Seems like it," I say. "The cop is knocking on doors, asking if anyone saw anything."

"Are you staying here?" asks Reece. "The smell of smoke is overpowering."

"I don't know what else to do," I say. "We'll just have to deal with it."

"I'll put that piece of plywood in the back over the broken window," says Reece, and he heads that way.

I turn on the TV and am surprised it works. As I'm trying to find the news, a van from an ABC affiliate pulls up in front of the house. A man with a camera pans the house as a reporter talks.

I go out the back door and around to the front. The reporter, a young blonde woman, waves and comes running. She recognizes me and draws to my side for an interview. I tell her what I know, and she asks if this could be related to Dahlia, and I say, "Yes."

Reece joins us to share his two cents. He explains he's not my husband, and the reporter finally understands. Finally satisfied, the reporter thanks us. Back inside, I grab the mop and start cleaning up the water. Reece places the couch and chair cushions outside on top of the shrubbery to dry. The front porch floor is charred, but you can still walk on it if you're careful. I have to call my Reece and let him know, but he doesn't answer. Fortunately, I snooped around on his phone and found Emma's number. I had planned on calling him and chewing him out, but I've compromised the relationship and feel guilty. I dial Emma's number. It rings forever before an older woman answers. I explain who I am and that it's an emergency. The phone clanks and bangs.

"Hello? How did you get this number? And what's the emergency?" he says. He sounds defiant.

"Someone tried to burn the house down. The whole front porch and the front part of the living room are wrecked. The news people came."

"Jesus, are you alright?"

"Yeah, just scared is all. What if they come back and finish the job?"

"Did you see anybody?"

"No, we came from Organon, and the front porch was

on fire."

"Who's we?"

I realize my mistake. "Reece came with me. Denise drove us. They were bored."

"Huh," he says. "So, I guess he's spending the night? That's weird."

"And you're spending the night at Emma's? Is that weird?"

We argue back and forth, forgetting about the fire. I learn that he, Emma, and Mia went to the zoo.

"Just having a good old time while the house burns," I say.

"And the mouse is at play while the cat's away," he says.

"Look, we need to talk when you get back, if you even plan to come back. Don't worry about us. We'll be fine. By the way, Rupert and Tweezer are okay, in case you forgot about them."

He sighs. "We'll leave soon and talk when we get back."

"You're just worried about Reece being here."

"Should I not be worried?"

"No more worried than I am, buster."

We leave it at that. Reece taps his fingers on the kitchen table. Despite the drama, I just want to hop in bed with him. There's an electric calm after the storm that wants to be fallen into.

"So, he's coming back tonight?" asks Reece.

"Yep."

"Should I be here? I'm afraid the shit will hit the fan." He stands and slides beside me, putting his arm around my waist. We have six hours, I remind him.

We take a good, long tumble in the guest bedroom. It's like we were made for each other. Reece says he thinks he's in love, and I return the sentiment. It's approaching midnight, and I suggest we sit in the living room, even though the couch is wet, and watch TV. The ceiling above the front window that broke is scorched, and the smell of smoke is powerful.

Headlights roam into the driveway, and I go to the back door and wait. I think I should run out and fall into his arms, but I can't do it. I stare at the yellow linoleum with faint hints of red and hear the back gate open. I open the door.

"You okay?" asks my Reece. He doesn't move in to hug me, as if asking about a paper cut.

"Is my room okay?" asks Mia.

"I'm fine, just smoky is all, and your room is fine," I say. I give Mia a hug. Reece looks frazzled, his hair askew. Mia runs into the living room and then up the stairs. I need her as a buffer, protection.

"Any idea who did it?" he says, sitting in a chair by the table. I know he knows Reece is here, but he's acting coy.

"No. Something to do with Dahlia, I'm sure. The police took a report. How was the drive?" I almost choke on my next words. "And how is our famous Emma in Alabama?"

"Oh brother," he says. "She's dandy, and that about sums it up."

"You took her to the zoo? You don't even like the zoo."

"Mia wanted to go." He rubs his head as if expecting electricity. "Where's Reece? In our bed?"

"Hey, now. Don't be rude. He's in the living room. I swear I saw a blue dot outside in the smoke. Dahlia may have been behind it, but Julia let it happen."

He ignores me. "I guess I should say hello to my younger twin."

He walks into the living room, looking at the ceiling as if Reece is not there. I follow, expecting the worst. Reece stands and puts his hands in his pockets, looking mighty guilty, and I wince. I've begun thinking of them as old and young Reece.

"Hey, what a mess," says young Reece. "I'll be able to help you clean up. Plenty of time on my hands."

"We'll be fine, I'm sure," says old Reece. "So, y'all just watching TV. The world is going to hell in a handbasket. Fascinating to watch, I'm sure, especially with a loved one."

"Reece, we're friends," I say without conviction.

"Pretty good friends, I'd say," he says. He takes a couple of steps toward young Reece.

"My books are okay!" yells Mia from the head of the stairs, and I yell back that's good news.

Without warning, old Reece dives for the leg of young Reece. I scream. He somehow gets behind Reece and has him in a bear hug. "The fuck," says young Reece, struggling. Old Reece throws him on top of the coffee table, and then they explode in a frenzy, knocking shit over. It strikes me they're wrestling and not hitting each other. They knock the TV off balance, and it slides to the floor, held up by the cord.

All I can do is yell, "Stop! Stop!"

Mia appears, her eyes wide. "Daddy! No!"

That stops the action, and both Reeces stand silent. "It's okay, honey," says old Reece. "Just a little playing around."

He's out of breath.

Mia runs to old Reece and hugs his leg. He pats her head and says that he's going to bed. "You guys can have the guest bedroom," he says to me.

"Reece, be real," I say. "He has to spend the night. Organon's entrance is closed."

"I'll sleep on the couch if you get me a blanket," says young Reece.

"Yeah, you do that," says old Reece, and he walks upstairs with Mia as if carrying a heavy load.

"You okay?" I say.

"Hurt my damn bicep, the motherfucker."

I can't help but say it. "I guess we got what we deserve."

Reece laughs and hugs me. "Something has to give, right? We were always meant to be together. It just got twisted, and he has a crush on the Alabama Emma."

"God, what a mess," I say. "The fire and this. Who knows what will happen next?"

He draws me close and says, "You have to make it happen with Reece. Be honest with him. Either way, we both have an Emma or a Reece, just not the right ones for now."

"What if I move into the guest facility with you? Or maybe we could get an apartment together?"

"I would love that," he says. "Let's talk to Dr. Markush about it."

I agree and fetch him a blanket and a dry pillow. When I check upstairs, Mia is in bed with Reece, so I head to the guest bedroom and sleep poorly, reliving the unwanted excitement of the day.

MULDRAUGH

I wake up early to noise in the street and look out the window, seeing three news vans with satellite dishes. I spot the mayor of Muldraugh, speaking with a reporter. The best I can tell, Town Hall supports Julia as the divine being of choice. The smell of smoke is still strong, and I open windows to air out the house. I hear shouts of "Emma!" and "Reece!" but ignore them. I'm not in the mood to look the part of the shaken victim. I peek in my bedroom, and Reece is awake, staring at the ceiling. He cuts his eyes my way, and I close the door. His cell phone rings, and I listen, but he doesn't answer. As I'm trotting down the stairs, my cell phone beeps. I see new Reece on the couch.

"Hello?"

"Emma, are you guys okay?" asks Markush. "Why didn't you call me and tell me about the fire? I saw it on the news this morning. For God's sake, this is serious. You could have died."

"Yeah, we're fine. Mia and Reece were away. It was on fire when we came home. Sorry about not calling. It was pure chaos."

"I didn't want any of you moving off base, precisely to avoid things like this. It's time everyone moves back, or we post a guard at your houses. I think moving back is the best option. Make sure you let Reece know."

"Yeah, for sure," I say. I tell him that old Reece and I are at a crossroads and that young Reece would move in with me if I asked him to.

"What?"

I tell him that new Reece and I have connected as soulmates and really believe it. He's stymied and says we must work out our problems the best we can, but the most critical issue now is safety. I agree and watch as new Reece sits up and makes space for me on the couch. I sit, and his thigh is against my thigh. Markush has to run, and I say bye.

"That was Markush," I say. I'm in my pajamas without a bra and worry that old Reece will come down and say something. "He wants us back on base, for safety."

"That sounds reasonable," says Reece. He looks cute shirtless and with his hair askew.

"I want us to stay together, me and you." A wave of panic washes over me as I realize what I'm saying.

Reece nods his head. "That would be great, if your Reece agrees."

On cue, old Reece ambles down the stairs. He walks to the window and sees the news vans. "Damn Dahlia is behind all this." He ignores us and pushes open the burned door. I can hear him yell "Fuck you!" and then his attention turns to us.

"Looking cozy," he says.

"Reece, we have to talk," I say. I tell him about Markush calling and wanting us to move back on base.

"I'm not going anywhere," he says. "Feel free to leave if you want. I'm sure you would like that." I feel threatened by him standing over us.

"Well, I'm going back," I say. "You can keep the car to take Mia to school."

"That's fine and dandy," he says and disappears into the kitchen. I hear the back door open and Reece talking with

Emma

Rupert, who has been barking off and on.

After an hour of uncomfortable silence, old Reece agrees to drive me and new Reece back to Organon. One of the news vans follows us, but gets stopped at the base gate. We ride without speaking, and I can tell that Mia is confused. I tell her I love her and that we'll see each other again. Reece pulls into the Organon parking lot, and young Reece hefts my suitcase out of the trunk.

"Have a great life," says old Reece.

"Take your meds," I say. He drives off without looking back.

Markush is in the day room on the medical unit, speaking with a returnee. We interrupt, and I tell him the situation, that old Reece is in love with Alabama Emma, and that young Reece and I will be staying in the guest facility. He's worried about Reece and Mia and says he will try to convince Reece to move back. I tell him that Reece has become increasingly paranoid and that he's not taking his meds. That worries him. I follow young Reece to the guest facility, feeling as though I'm walking down a long hallway to board a plane for who knows where.

"Well, you have finally returned!" says Caroline. "I've been so alone. I've wanted to summon Herr Schopenhauer."

"How could we forget you?" asks Reece with some sincerity.

I'd almost forgotten about Caroline. "Hey, sorry about that. I'm staying here for a while so we can catch up. Your hair looks nice."

"Thank you, dear. I've used what you call shampoo

with wonderful results." Caroline wears a poker face but becomes animated when she talks. I think she thinks that this Reece is my Reece, and she doesn't ask why I'm staying here, but I explain, and she seems amused more than anything. "Young love is mysterious," she says.

I glance at the TV, and they're talking about the upcoming debate between the Republican, Democratic, and Independent candidates. There is plenty to like about the incumbent, Lowell Beatty, but he's getting up in years and has a clear agenda for Dahlia. The republican, Thomas Crinkle, is an outright idiot. For him, everything about the current administration is "real bad" or "terrible, just terrible." The fear is that his billions will put him in office.

I have to catch myself from going down a rabbit hole. Reece takes my suitcase and puts it in a room, and I ask Caroline if she would like to go shopping on the Organon dime. She brightens and says that she must freshen up. It's only ten, and we have plenty of time. Markush has given old Reece and me the day off due to the fire. To be safe, we take new Reece with us. It's probably best if we stay on base, but I don't think the PX will have what Caroline needs. I realize we don't have a car, and have to bite the bullet and ask Markush for his old Volvo. He's not happy about it but relents, saying that Denise can take him home to retrieve his Jaguar. While waiting on Caroline, I get calls from Arthur and Afewerki, who have seen news of the fire on TV.

By ten-thirty, we're on our way. The inside of the Volvo smells like diesel, and the engine rattles. It's a windy day, but pleasant at fifty degrees, and we head to nearby Radcliff to Topp's Dress Shop. The shopping center park-

Emma

ing lot is crowded, and there are cars with "Julia" painted on the back windows. In front of a department store are supporters of Dahlia and The Truth Ranch collecting donations. We enter the warm Topp's, and there are dresses galore with underthings and hats.

Caroline thumbs a rack of dresses and moves to the wall, where there are some long dresses, which I imagine she prefers. I spot a red bodycon and hold it up for her. She laughs and points to a dark yellow drop-waist that would fall below her knees and not reveal her curves. Being a seamstress by profession, she examines it carefully, scrutinizing the seams and the gathering at the bottom.

"I'm not familiar with the stitching," she says. "It seems rather weak, but I do like it."

"Reece, what do you think?" I say. He's on the edge of boredom, I can tell.

"Looks good. Try it on," he says.

I help her pick out a size ten, and show her how to use the dressing room. She takes forever but finally emerges. The dress fits her fine in the waist, but I realize that her boobs are much larger than I thought. With a bra, she'll bust out at the top. She seems slightly embarrassed at Reece's presence and tries on the same dress, but a size bigger.

Caroline examines herself in the mirror. "With a bit of sewing in the waist, this will do just fine. Do you think that Arthur would approve?"

"His eyes will pop out," says Reece with a grin, and I laugh.

"Can you sew?" I say.

"Why, of course," she says, "but I need thread, a thimble, and scissors, if we can locate those items."

I pay for the dress, only fifty bucks, and convince her to get a bra and socks as well. Her shoes seem sturdy, but are worn and old-fashioned. Reece runs the purchases to the car, and we head to the department store. We have to walk by the small group collecting donations for Dahlia and keep our heads down. They grow quiet as we pass, and we enter the vast store with its high ceilings.

"My goodness!" says Caroline, lingering at a jewelry counter.

We let her look and admire the goods, finally arriving at the sewing supplies. She gathers what she needs and then ogles the toothpaste aisle, examining each item. I explain toothpaste, and she says that she used baking soda back home. Finally, we check out, and I'm worried about the people outside. I tell Reece that we should be careful, and he flexes his bicep. He looks cute in his hiking shorts and long-sleeve t-shirt. We exit.

"Well, if it ain't some clowns from Organon," says a chunky woman with black bangs. "Care to donate to the true God?"

The woman is sipping from a cup of ice. I want to disappear, but stand my ground with Reece beside me. Caroline senses danger and moves away from the group.

"Y'all have a good day," says Reece. I can tell he's amped and holding back. I notice the blue dot floating above their small table, where a plastic bowl contains bills and change.

"Don't tell us what to do, moron," says the chunky woman. Suddenly, she throws the cup of ice in my face. Reece reacts and slaps the cup out of her hand.

Emma

"Bitch, get a life," says Reece. I tug on his arm and lead him away, wiping water off my face, and Caroline takes his place with her hands on her hips.

"Mind your manners, young lady," says Caroline.

The woman hesitates, then charges Caroline, chest out, and bumps her. The other three look sheepish with their arms crossed. "Dahlia does not forgive you," says Chunky. "Either get right or get left."

"Humph," says Caroline, holding her bag of sewing supplies. "Dahlia is a spoiled brat who creates only harm. One must recognize Julia as the true power." She sounds convincing and doesn't give Chunky an inch.

"We're out of here," says Reece. "Let's go." He takes my hand, which is nice, and Caroline follows us to the car.

The old Volvo sputters, then cranks. "Damn idiots," says Reece. "They're probably the ones who tried to burn your house down."

"Every time we leave base, something happens," I say.

"Yeah, Markush will say told you so," he says.

"I am in need of fresh air," says Caroline. "The guest facility is cloying and tedious."

"You could move in with Arthur," says Reece with a grin.

"Do you think so?" she says. "I wonder if he would behave as a gentleman."

"I'm positive he would be the perfect gentleman," I say. "He's as solid as a rock, although a little moody sometimes."

We arrive back at Organon and meet two returnees, heading out after their evaluations. We let Caroline put her things away, and she changes into the new dress before altering it. I've called Arthur and he's excited that we will come over.

Caroline takes the lead. Her clogs look a little strange with the dress, and I decide that will be our next outing, shoe shopping.

"Is this the door?" she says, and she knocks before I can answer.

Arthur takes his time answering the door, but is all smiles. "Welcome, my friends! So good to see you. Caroline, what a fetching dress."

"Well, thank you. I'm flattered. Emma helped me to choose. There's some adjustments to be had, but it fits nicely as a ready-made."

Arthur's white hair is a wild mess, combed straight back. He has volume. But he's cleanly shaved and looks deceptively youthful.

"The fire, the fire," says Arthur. "I'm thankful no one was injured. What a fright."

"Yeah, a real mess," I say.

"Come and seat yourselves," says Arthur. "I shall provide an afternoon libation acquired by Dr. Markush, Strothmann Weizenkorn." He heads to the kitchen without asking if we want what is basically vodka at two o'clock.

"Such a nice apartment," says Caroline. "How many bedrooms are there?" She lowers her voice.

"Just one, I think," I say.

"Oh my," says Caroline. "Perhaps he would sleep on this ample couch."

"You should ask," says Reece. I can tell that he's trying to stir up some trouble.

Arthur returns with a tray and four tumblers filled with an inch of clear liquid. We watch in silence as he doles out the shots to us.

"Not so strong," says Arthur. He takes a sip as Reece and I down our portions. The alcohol burns my throat, and I cough. Like Arthur, Caroline is sipping. She tells him about our shopping adventure. I can tell she wants to ask him about the bedroom.

"Another taste?" asks Arthur, and Reece and I decline.

"You know, my dear man, that drinking so early is not healthy," says Caroline. "It's going straight to my head." I'm waiting, and so is Reece. "Which reminds me that my living conditions are unsuitable. I would so like to join you, Arthur, if it pleases you." I can't wait for the response.

Arthur coughs. "Yes, I see. Perhaps you could stay with Dr. Markush. He has two bedrooms." He's acting clueless, but maybe he is clueless.

"I don't want you to leave me again," she says.

"Maybe you could sleep on the couch," says Reece.

"Me?" asks Caroline. "Why me? I am a lady."

Arthur downs his Strothmann's and hurries to the kitchen for the bottle.

"Caroline, give him time to think about it. He's a cranky old man and set in his ways," I say.

"Yes, perhaps you are right. But I get so lonely."

Arthur acts as if he's escaped a trap and takes a seat. Reece and I look at each other and laugh.

"There is an empty apartment, just next door," says Arthur.

"What? And be all alone?" Caroline looks miffed.

"You would be right next to Arthur," I say. "You could have tea parties."

Caroline resists, but we convince her that she'll be happier if she moves out of Organon.

FORT KNOX

It's a week later, and I've not spoken with old Reece. I'm not sure what he's up to other than putting up cameras. I do miss him and Mia, but young Reece and I are meant to be together, and Reece has practically shacked up with Alabama Emma. There's the problem that we're still married, but that's a quick fix.

Caroline has moved into the empty apartment and is driving Arthur a little bit crazy. I can tell he likes her, especially since she is twenty years his junior. He seems to be in disbelief at the situation and doesn't know how to handle it. They've taken to walking around the lake together, which is cute.

The world is in turmoil, even here on base, where there have been confrontations in the housing complexes. The cops and jailers had it easy for a while, but business has picked back up. Around the country, followers of the Julia and Dahlia camps have taken over city parks with tents and signs. There was a battle that broke out in Racine, Wisconsin, with dozens of protesters injured. The presidential debate is tomorrow night, and we can't wait to see our man Steven MacGivelry, the Independent candidate, debating that doofus Crinkle and the incumbent Harry Sheets.

The good news is that I'm staying in Organon's guest facility with Reece. We have the place to ourselves, and we're using it well, although we're bored most of the time. I've discovered that Reece likes his back scratched as a kind of foreplay. He bends and twists and moans and tells me to draw blood. He gets pretty worked up, which is amusing. A stone table and two stout chairs sit outside the front of Organon, but inside the barbed wire. It's after lunch, turkey subs and potato salad, and Reece and I sit in the sun.

"I wonder what Reece is up to?" I say, meaning old Reece.

"You know as well as I do," says Reece.

And then, just like magic, my cell phone rings, and it's Reece.

"Hey," I say.

"Just checking in," he says. "The carpenters have about finished with the porch, and I've got the place lit up with cameras. How are you?"

"I'm fine. Reece is here with me, sitting in the sun."

"We need to talk. What's going on?"

"Yeah, need to talk."

"So, what the hell are we doing? I know that you and Reece have consummated your love, which is basically adultery."

"How do I know what you did with Alabama Emma on your little trip?" I know I'm not being helpful, but feel penned in a corner.

"Well, we didn't hop in the sack. Mia was with me, and she really likes Emma."

"So, I'm not good enough to be Mia's mother?" The writing is on the wall, but I can't bring myself to say that it's over between us. I want him to say it.

"I didn't say that. She loves you. But we're heading down a path that features no turning back. Maybe we shouldn't have rushed to get married." I look at Reece, and he's nodding his head. He can hear.

"Yeah," I say. "We can't travel universes and then get stuck. Anything can happen, and it is happening."

"I'm taking my meds and feel a lot better. I was staying up all night, watching the yard."

"That's good. Why didn't you do that for me? I guess the other Emma is a better influence than I am."

"She was a psych nurse for ten years and knows. Yeah, she convinced me. Said it wouldn't work out if I stayed unmedicated."

"Do you love her?" I say. There is a long pause.

"Yes, I do. Do you love Reece, the oh-so-young version of me?"

I don't want to say it, but have to. "I do."

"Well, then it's settled. We go our separate ways," he says.

"Right. I suppose that is what we do." I'm relieved and excited that I can be more open with young Reece. He changes the subject.

"I talked with Kristin, and she's a mess. She can't get past the car bombing and fears for her life and Dahlia's."

"Wow. What exactly is she doing?" I say.

"She's become one of Simon Klinefelter's wives, but is the top dog. She sits on a kind of throne all day with Dahlia, receiving visitors and giving blessings."

"That's very weird," I say.

"Yeah, she's trapped there and wants to get out. Dahlia seems to be becoming more human each day. Kristin says that she's stopped her little pranks, that she's losing her powers."

"Hmm," I say. "That's a good thing. Good for Julia."

We talk for a few more minutes and say goodbye. It

feels like the last time I'll talk to him. I give Reece the rundown of what Reece said.

"Sounds like Kristin is cracking under the weight," he says. "What will happen next?"

"I have no idea. She's supposed to be at the rally in DC," I say.

"And we're still going, right? Maybe we'll see Kristin and Dahlia there."

"Yeah," I say.

"Should be exciting. Are Reece and Mia going?"

"I don't know. Not with us anyway," I say.

We soak up the sun, chatting, and Markush arrives at the gate. He looks frazzled, his hair in need of a wash.

"Hey, guys!" he says. "Getting some sun, I see." He's wearing a gray blazer and black suit pants.

"What's up?" I say.

"Just doing some interviews. We have two new returnees arriving later today, from Texas and Arkansas.

I tell him about the shopping fiasco, and he looks concerned, saying that we need to stay on base. He's worried about the other Emma and Reece and wants them to move back from Radcliff. I briefly mention the call with old Reece and Kristin's situation. He thinks that Kristin will return, but I'm not so sure.

"Alright, on my way," says Markush, leaving us in the sun.

"I wonder if Kristin misses Reece," says Reece.

"That would complicate things. He'll never leave Alabama-Emma," I say.

"What about us? Where do we stand now? It looks like we have free rein," he says.

Emma

"We're good," I say. "Do you think it's not good?"

"No, I think we're excellent. We've traveled the universes to be with each other, plus we can have kids," he says.

That shocks me. I haven't been thinking about kids just yet, although I've always wanted a little boy. Reece will make a great father.

"Yeah, kids," I say. "But not too soon. Do you love me?" My heart skips a beat.

He grabs my hand. "Oh boy, I love you lots and lots, baby. We're perfect together."

That makes me giddy, and I smile, squeezing his hand.

"Look at that," says Reece. He points. It's Caroline and Arthur, 'perambulating' as he would say. She's holding his right arm with both hands, like something from a movie.

"Call them over," I say. "They're so cute."

"Hey, Arthur!" says Reece. He stands and walks to the gate.

"Yes, hello! We are perambulating in this fine weather," says Arthur as he slips from the grip of Caroline.

"Won't you join us?" asks Caroline. She's wearing her new dress, and she needs more.

Reece hits the red button, and the gate opens. "Where you headed?"

"Just the lake, my good friend," says Arthur. He looks youthful, having shaved and trimmed back his mutton chops. "Yes, you should join us by all means."

"Spending some quality time together, I see." We head for the north side of the lake on the main road.

"Indeed," says Arthur. "Although I am preparing for a lecture on transcendental technology. I find it fascinating that so much progress has been made and wish to explain it in terms of idealism."

"Oh, your silly lectures," says Caroline. She tries to take his hand, but he avoids the clasp. "I think we are what matters most, trapped in this strange land."

"Yes, dear," says Arthur. "But I must be prepared."

"Where's the lecture?" asks Reece.

"My premiere lecture will take place at Eastern Kentucky University, the college where our friend Afewerki studies and where the other Reece taught philosophy. After that, we will see what happens with Harvard and Yale. I'm looking most forward to my trip to Berlin, which will take place in September, I believe."

"Cool," I say, and Reece as well.

"And I must travel with you, dear sir, especially to Berlin, where I long to be," says Caroline.

"You would be bored, my dear," says Arthur.

"No, no! You are a statesman and need a lady at your side," says Caroline.

"Sounds like you don't have a choice, Arthur," says Reece.

"We shall see," says Arthur.

We reach the dirt roads and head that way. It's so amusing to watch Caroline dote on Arthur. He is the definition of reluctance with some pride mixed in.

"I hesitate to ask, but where is your Reece?" Arthur says to me.

"We're taking a break. This right here is my real Reece." I slap Reece on the butt, and he gives me a noogie.

"Dear me, that is news. He is alone with Mia?" asks Arthur.

"Yep," I say.

Emma

"It's a crazy world said the psychiatrist orbiting the Earth in a yellow canoe." Reece laughs, and we all look stymied.

FORT KNOX

It's Tuesday, and the presidential debate is tonight. Across the country, turmoil continues primarily between Dahlia's and Julia's supporters. National Guards in some states, such as Alabama and Oregon, have taken sides, coming out in force. A state of national emergency was declared yesterday, which seems overdue.

I worked the day shift at Organon, and it's strange to see old Reece there. He seems happy and friendly with no discussion of our situation. I lunched with young Reece afterward in the guest facility, and then there was a little kissing action. We have the place to ourselves except for when Donna vacuums or the lunch ladies bring our meal trays. Markush says he'll acquire another car for Reece and me to use and shuttle around Caroline and Arthur. The debate starts at seven, and Markush says he will join us and bring snacks and beer.

The time arrives, and we're glued to the TV, munching on microwave popcorn and drinking Bud Light. The stage is lit with three podiums against a satin blue background. Two moderators introduce the debate and the rules. There is a minute of shuffling, and the candidates emerge and take their places. Our man, Steven MacGivelry, the Independent candidate, looks sharp and arranges a notepad. The Republican Thomas Crinkle looks angry with a smirk, and the incumbent Harry Sheets, who is eighty, appears to have lost something. No one shakes hands, all looking straight ahead as if scouting for a train, and the broadcast goes to a drain cleaner commercial.

The debate is back, and the first question is "How will you incorporate Julia or Dahlia as deities to be worshipped? We'll start with Mr. Crinkle, then President Sheets, and then Mr. MacGivelry. You have two minutes to respond."

Crinkle hunches over, a swoosh of yellow hair floating on his head. His eyes squint from a long face. "First, the current administration is terrible, absolutely the worst presidency in the history of the world. Second, Julia and Dahlia are jokes. The American people need to follow the one true God. Julia and Dahlia are shams. They're just terrible and cause terrible things. Look at the shooting in Las Vegas and the car bombing in California. That is terrible. The country is in a shambles, and mass confusion is the rule of order. If needed, there will be war. I promise. It's just really terrible."

There's a slight pause, and the camera goes to Sheets, who is shaking his head. He is old and looks old. He appears to have his act together, but occasionally gets lost in his speech. "There is certainly turmoil in the land, and our primary focus will be to ease that turmoil and restore peace. Our position is that Dahlia embodies what has historically made our country great—hardworking people striving to make the dream a reality. Dahlia reigned for an eternity, allowing people to fail and suffer the cruel vagaries of life. That suffering, though, is key to making us the human beings that we are. Julia is a pipe dream. There have been unusual decreases in crime and incidents of disease and injury, but we believe that to be an outcome of Dahlia, not Julia. Our traditional God has been Dahlia all along."

He drones on for another minute, and then MacGivelry is in the spotlight. He looks confident with his thick, dark gray hair combed back. "Dear people, the unrest in our country is unprecedented. Not since the Civil War have we had such polarity. Our current president would have us descend into further chaos, dividing the country. The one true God is Julia. She's the one who has brought us the health and well-being that looms above the madness. She has, in the past months, though, allowed conflicts to fester and play out, sometimes ending in violence. Julia recognizes the need to defeat the influence of Dahlia and remove her from what is becoming bedlam."

"He's very convincing," says Reece.

"Can't wait to hear what Crinkle has to say," says Markush. We're on our second beer, watching a dog food commercial. The debate returns.

Crinkle grips the podium and leans into it like a mighty wind will carry him away. "Dahlia is terrible. Julia is terrible. It's really terrible."

One of the moderators asks him to speak only when called upon, and Crinkle flashes a sour face. After discussing the economy, which is "terrible, the worst ever," the candidates are asked about a pending Supreme Court decision on an amendment to the Constitution that would recognize Dahlia as the true god. Crinkle and MacGivelry are against the idea, and a brief spat erupts between all three, which ends with the moderators calling for calm. The next question is, "National Guard units are defecting to Julia. What is your plan to deal with the National Guard?"

"Their behavior is terrible," says Crinkle. "I will send

in armed forces to squash this terrible situation. We must stay strong and unified as a nation. Julia is just dust in the wind. She's ridiculous and terrible. I don't even like to say her name. There is one true God, and we will, if necessary, defund any efforts that put our God in danger. No more money for the terrible people who have terrible ideas." He is finally stopped, and MacGivelry speaks.

"To each his own," says MacGivelry. "Julia is the true God. She is in control. Dahlia, at this point, is a mere puppet. We beseech the National Guard units to unify against the forces of darkness and recognize Julia as our beneficent queen. I hate to be with Mr. Crinkle, but armed regular forces may need to be called in to restore order. Julia wants peace but has no patience for Dahlia and her schemes."

Sheets has been listening but straining to hear, looking a little bewildered. "We have ordered National Guard units to remain neutral. Units that choose sides will be dealt with on a state-by-state basis." His speech is slightly slurred, and his voice trails off at the end of his sentences.

"We have Sheets to blame for the uproar," says Crinkle. "He's a terrible leader, just absolutely terrible."

We laugh every time he says "terrible." It's a good thing we're not doing shots every time he says "terrible."

The debate lasts about an hour and a half, and we eat a frozen pizza, plus the chips and dip Markush brought. We've killed the six-pack and have resorted to sweet tea. The TV flickers, and slowly the face of a little girl appears. It's Julia, and we stop talking.

"Hello, people. I've enjoyed hearing your leaders speak, but you must know that Dahlia has chosen to become human, and she has no real powers any longer." Her face glows, and she fades to brief static before returning to the debate. The moderators seem confused and listen to a producer who tells them what just happened. The camera switches to a newsroom where a pretty lady with high cheekbones is excited by the appearance of Julia, but after a commercial, the debate returns for a last question.

"Wow," I say. "Dahlia no longer has powers, if I heard correctly."

"I think you did," says Reece.

"That was great for MacGivelry. Sheets is too old, and Crinkle is just plain crazy," says Markush.

The three candidates resemble soldiers in battle, bracing for the next missile to drop. The moderators play their roles as dead serious as possible. "What is your stance on raising taxes to help reduce the national debt? Mr. Crinkle, your response."

Crinkle pumps his large head and re-grips the podium. "Yes, lower taxes for all, unprecedented lower taxes. I have a wonderful plan to make the American people richer. What we have now is terrible, just terrible. Comrade Sheets wants to gouge those who have worked hard for their millions, which is terrible for the economy. What's most important are tariffs. Our country is being raped by countries like Canada and China. I will make them pay their fair share and increase the wealth of our country while reducing the national debt. A wonderful, wonderful plan."

"I'll respond," says Sheets. He shuffles paper and looks somewhat lost. "Crinkle here wants to give tax breaks to the rich and increase corporate wealth through tariffs.

It's all about stroking the rich and ignoring the poor and middle class." He loses his train of thought and looks confused. "His plan is 'terrible' and will result in more global unrest. If we want to make the United States a laughingstock of the world, then pump up the tariffs."

Crinkle starts to speak, but is interrupted by a moderator. "Mr. McGivelry, your response please."

We listen, and he wants to walk a line between Sheets and Crinkle, whom he calls radicals. He says he'll reduce taxes for all at a fair rate across the board, giving everybody a bigger piece of the pie, which sounds reasonable. He doesn't say much about tariffs, other than he will make sure that this country is treated fairly. He starts to talk about human rights, and a moderator reins him in for final comments. We've had enough, so we turn down the volume.

"Crinkle is truly 'terrible', and Sheets is cruising into dementia," says Markush. "It'll be a close one for sure."

Reece and I agree with him. During the debate, I managed to melt into him, but now my neck hurts, and I sit up. Reece leans forward, and I scratch his back. Markush knows about the big switch between us and doesn't bat an eye. He suddenly lays some news on us.

"Got a call from Kristin, and she's a mess."

"What happened?" I say.

"The guy who runs the Truth Ranch, Simon, wants to officially marry her, and Kristin says no way. He wants to form a trinity between himself, Dahlia, and Kristin."

"Is Kristin going to leave?" asks Reece. He puts his feet on the coffee table next to the chips.

"Well, there's more," says Markush. "Simon wants to

have sex with Dahlia to make himself divine. He's a real psychopath, very manipulative. Frankly, I feel bad for Dahlia. She's lost her powers and is stuck with people who only want to use her."

"Gosh," I say. "We need to bring them back. That's disgusting."

"She's on the fence," says Markush. "But I told her she's welcome to come back here. I really wish she would, for her and Dahlia's safety."

"Should we go and get them?" I say.

"I wouldn't go that far," says Markush. "She has this vision of herself as a special being in charge of Dahlia. She still has the Organon credit card, which she can use to buy a ticket if she chooses. I hate to say it, but I've asked Julia to watch out for her."

"I get it," I say. "It's hard to take a seven-year-old girl seriously."

"Oh, and I heard from Reece, your, umm, husband. He's going to move to Alabama to be with the Emma there. He plans to leave as soon as school is out, which is this month. Did you know?"

"No," I say, feeling sad. We've split up, but I still care about him. "I guess it was just meant to be, crisscrossing universes to find a true self."

"You guys can have the house in Muldraugh if he actually leaves," says Markush. "Unless you like it here."

Reece and I glance at one another and nod. We would like that very much, despite the safety issues. The house, now has cameras and alarms, partially thanks to Reece's paranoia. It's past nine, and Markush says he has to run.

Emma

He has a flight to D.C. at noon tomorrow. The news is showing a riot in Little Rock, Arkansas, and we turn up the volume.

MULDRAUGH

A couple of weeks have passed. Reece and I live in the house, which still smells like smoke, but the front porch has been fixed. The old Reece moved out with Mia a few days ago, as school was over. He took practically nothing, just clothes and a knife he likes. Markush asked him to leave the car for us, and he and Mia were shuttled to Alabama in a Humvee. Afewerki is out of school for ten days and is staying with us. He's so funny about smells and dislikes the charred wood odor. Reece and I are working half-day shifts at Organon as usual.

It's two-thirty, and Reece and I lounge on the couch, watching the news, which we do with frequency. I'm confused by the alliances being made between National Guard units and militias. The country is a wreck and could go down at any moment, it seems. Armed troops have arrived in Little Rock to quell violence between supporters of Julia and Dahlia. It's just getting nasty. If all hell breaks loose, Markush wants us to return to base and live within the walls of Organon.

"Julia needs to show her skills if she wants Dahlia's folks to come to the light," says Reece.

"Maybe another TV spot or changing water into wine," I say. He laughs, and I give him a big side hug.

Afewerki joins us, looking sheepish. "I am not understanding. Your husband has left."

"He's in love with Alabama Emma, and I'm in love with Reece here. I know it seems strange, but it's for the best. "Am I right?"

Reece nods and kisses me, making Afewerki wince. He's not much for public displays of affection.

"You are divor-ced?" asks Afewerki.

"Not yet, but soon," I say.

"It's Julia's will," says Reece. "She made it happen, although Dahlia put the gears in motion."

I switch the TV to camera mode for a minute. Rupert is asleep in the backyard. The front porch is clear. We watch the four screens as if in a trance, with nothing happening.

"What's for dinner?" I say and rub Reece's thigh. Afewerki, have you been to the Chinese place in Radcliff?"

"No, I have not been there." He plays with his Exxon cap. "Is it good, the Chinese food?"

"Yeah, you can get something spicy if you want," says Reece.

"Yes, I would like to try," says Afewerki.

I go back to the news and it's live coverage of a Julia march in New York City. The group of three hundred or so has stopped in Times Square, chanting beneath the electric lights. Police with riot gear line the streets. There are "Julia=Love" posters and one that says "Poor Dahlia." When I think of NYC, I can only remember the pee smell in the subways.

We get caught up in the news like zombies, and before you know it, it's hitting five o'clock. We decide to do an early dinner to beat the rush. The drive is uneventful, although we pass small groups holding signs. Great China Wall sits beside a strip mall and is quite large. It's a buffet with probably a hundred choices. I help Afewerki with his selections, steering him to the Kung Pao chicken, which has three peppers on the sign. He gets four eggrolls, and I laugh at him.

"How are your studies going?" I say.

Afewerki is dipping his egg rolls in red sauce and seems satisfied. "It is going very well. We are studying homicide investigation and also mental illness. It is complex. People with mental illness are to be more likely to be a victim of crime, yet they also commit many crimes. I had not thought of this before."

We agree that's interesting, and then he complains about his roommate, who is still afraid of him. Afewerki would like to live alone, and we promise to put in a good word with Markush. Afewerki has never been to a buffet before and is amazed that he can go back for seconds and thirds, which he does. He says that he's lost weight and complains about the food in the university cafeteria as being very bland. He does not like salad, that's for sure. Absolutely stuffed, we head back to the house, but I have a little errand.

"Stop at Pookie's Pharmacy," I say to Reece, who is driving.

"What for?" asks Reece.

"Oh, just a little something for us. Afewerki, you need anything?"

He says, "No," and Reece heads for Pookie's, run by an old pharmacist, Dr. Pookie himself.

Reece parks. The evening is cool and bright with puffy clouds taped to the sky. I run in and spot what I need, then get a gourmet chocolate bar to share with the guys. It takes forever to pay, as I shift from one foot to the other. Back in the saddle, we head home, and there are three people with Julia signs in front of the house. We don't mind having them, but they attract attention. Reece pulls deep into the driveway, and we enter through the back door after playing with Rupert for a few minutes.

Inside, I trot to the bathroom, leaving the guys to eat the chocolate bar at the kitchen table. With the door closed and the fan on, I drop my drawers and pee on the plastic stick. My heart is in my throat as I sit there, pants down, staring as the double lines slowly appear. Yep, I'm pregnant, and it has to be with young Reece. We both have the same number of chromosomes, twenty-eight pairs.

I feel like my face is flushed, and I feel a bit shaky. I want to shout out the news, but am hesitant. What does it all mean? I'm having Reece's baby. Will he run like a scared deer? I decide to wait until we're alone, feeling a little sick. We gather in the living room and automatically turn on the TV. Wall Street has been inundated with protestors, and tensions are high. The National Guard is on the scene, but it's reported that the outfit is divided over who to support. I decide to steer the conversation toward work as I bite my nails.

"That Michael Fleer is a real character," I say. Fleer is a new arrival at Organon, accompanied by his daughter, Felicity.

"Yeah, in a coma for six years. He can barely stand," says Reece.

I give some details for the benefit of Afewerki. "He talked about being in Ethiopia, looking for his daughter. He says that he met a Reece and Emma, but they were not of much use. The village was bizarre with a pink sky and herds of wild pigs that the people avoided like the plague, believing them to hold dead souls.

"This is very strange," says Afewerki. "In my country, the pig is unclean and does not exist, just the goats and sheep and cows."

"Fleer wants reparations for lost wages and compensation for his pain and turmoil. He says the government owes him millions for his troubles," I say.

"He's not the only one," says Reece. "It's like a movement. Dahlia was at fault, but you can't sue Dahlia, or maybe you can."

"The government is supporting Dahlia," says Afewerki.

"Yeah, they seem culpable," says Reece. "I would like some of that reparation myself, although we've got it pretty good."

I'm dying to tell Reece the news and snuggle into him, dropping a leg over his. On TV, scenes play of teargas canisters smoking and young people throwing bricks. I wonder where they got the bricks.

"It's endless," says Reece. He puts his hand behind my head and draws me in for a kiss. Afewerki squirms and excuses himself, saying that he must study, although he's out of school for the summer. We wish him a good night and stretch out side by side on the couch, which is still damp and smoky.

Reece turns up the TV volume, and now is the time, but I can't bring myself to say it. It's hard to believe there's a baby growing inside of me. A reporter is speaking with a man who has a large cut on his forehead with blood dripping into his mouth. Is this the kind of world to bring a baby into?

"I'll be right back," I say, and I run to the kitchen. I call Reece on his cell phone.

"Hello?" he says.

"Hey, soldier, I'm in the kitchen." My heart is in my throat, beating solid.

"Yeah, okay. What's up with the phone call?"

"Got some news for you." My head feels like a balloon.

"What?"

"Well, I'm pregnant." He doesn't say anything, and I'm worried he's angry. I'm pressing the phone to my ear. "Reece?"

He walks into the kitchen with his arms open wide, and I rush into them. He squeezes me and says, "I love you."

"I love you too. What do you think?" He relaxes his grip on me.

"It's the best news ever. I can't believe it. Wow, a baby." He plants a big kiss on the top of my head. One thing I like about him is that he's taller and I have to look up. "Can we tell people?"

"Maybe not yet. Let me get tested at the hospital to make sure. I'm thrilled," I say.

"Yeah, me too. I can't wait to tell my grandparents. We'll go see them and tell them in person."

"Sounds good," I say. "Gosh, I don't know what to do. I feel like I'm at the edge of a high dive, and I'm afraid of heights." We embrace and kiss, and I feel his warmth, his sameness. There's nothing to do but head back to the couch, where there's an update on the riots in Little Rock. We settle into each other like old friends, and he scratches my arm, which I like.

"You still okay to go to the gathering in D.C.? It's on Saturday," he says.

"I don't know. Do you think there'll be violence?"

"Yeah, for sure, but it's important that Julia has the best turnout. I'll protect you."

"I appreciate that, soldier. Let me think about it, though. It is a baby for Christ's sake."

"Right, our baby," he says.

My cell phone rings, and it's Arthur. He never calls me. "Hey, Arthur, what's up?" I slide out from beneath Reece's arm and lean forward. He says that Caroline is being a pest and won't leave him alone. He wants to know what he should do. I can hear her babbling in the background, so she must be in his apartment. I give Reece my best bug eyes and tell Arthur that he should be patient, that Caroline is quite the catch, especially for a man of his age. She's proof of his own world, and he needs to hold onto her. "You need each other," I say. He's at his wits' end, and I can't help laughing at him. He sounds like a little girl complaining that the cat is messing with her dolls. "Just treat her like a lady, a delicate lady, and see what happens." He mumbles and then hangs up.

"What was that all about?" asks Reece. "Arthur getting cold feet?"

"Yeah, Caroline is hinting at marriage, and he's freaking out. She requires a lot of attention."

"It's good for him. He needs a partner in crime. I know that he's attracted to her, but he's stubborn."

"What if Caroline gets pregnant?" I say.

"That would take the cake." We both laugh, and I hit Reece on the arm. He puts me in a loose headlock and rubs my hair. We wrestle for a minute and wind up side by side, breathing into each other's faces.

WASHINGTON D.C.

Markush has strictly forbidden us from attending the big rally in D.C., but everyone will be there, including supporters of Julia, Dahlia, and traditional Gods. Reece and I have convinced Caroline and Arthur to join us. Arthur is frantic about Caroline and thinks this will give her something else to think about, plus he's never been to D.C. I don't tell him about Markush and his order to stay home. I check in with the other Reece and Emma, and they're going to sit this one out. We don't have room in the car anyway, and Afewerki is just plain frightened to go. It's a ten-hour drive from Muldraugh, and we'll arrive Friday night and stay at a motel in Maryland at a Red Carpet Inn in Indian Head. That's as close as we can get. We don't take signs and have a plan to play it neutral, just absorbing the experience. It's really quite exciting as we leave Fort Knox, having picked up Arthur and Caroline, who is wearing a new sleeveless dress of linen that she tailored herself. She says it's perfect for hot weather. I want to tell them I'm pregnant, but am waiting to see the doctor.

Just ten minutes into the drive, Caroline starts singing in German. She and Reece have the back seat, I'm driving, and Arthur is up front with me as he is quite bulky.

"Such an inane song and bad poetry," says Arthur. He shakes his head, gazing at the scenery, woods, and pastureland.

"I will have you know that my mother taught me that song," says Caroline.

"I like it," says Reece.

"Thank you," says Caroline. She takes it down a notch but continues to sing.

It's a cloudy day with a purple glow to the west. There was talk of tornado weather on the news. We're on I-64 and have passed through Lexington, where protesters have gathered on bridges, signs hanging from the railings. The closer we get to D.C., the more anxious I become, expecting the worst. We could be arrested or even hurt.

"A pottery barn," says Arthur, scanning the surroundings. "I suppose one would find pottery there."

"Yes, pottery in a barn," says Reece, laughing.

It's raining now and very dim. The skies are dirty white with patches of black. At one o'clock, we exit and visit a McDonald's, which is new for Caroline. I explain to her the global reach of McDonald's, that you can visit just about any country and find one. Caroline is at a loss as to what to order, and I suggest the Big Mac, but then think she might not like having to open her mouth so wide. She settles on the fish filet, and Arthur gets the quarter-pounder. Reece and I have the Big Mac combos. The mood is pleasant, but there's an unknown that we all seem to be worried about.

The rain hits harder and harder, and Caroline is afraid. I do slow down, but can barely see the lights of the semi in front of me. Inside, the sound is loud and menacing. Traffic slows and is backed up just before the West Virginia border. It takes us an hour to go four miles, and we see what the problem is. Traffic is being stopped by state troopers for some reason. Finally, it's our turn, and I power down the window. The trooper is wearing a full-body rain slicker and looks frazzled. He gets right to the point.

"Any weapons on board: guns, knives, explosives?"

"No sir," I say.

He gazes in the back seat. "Where you headed?"

"D.C., to the rally."

"You might as well turn around. You'll never get through. Pop the trunk and hood for me." I do, and he quickly peers into both. "You're good to go and be safe."

Caroline needs the ladies' room, and we proceed to the rest area just ahead. The parking lot is full, and I park along a curb. Some cars have Julia or Dahlia painted on their back windshields, and even here, I can feel tension. Back in the car, Reece takes over for the rest of the drive as I relax in the back with Caroline. Traffic soon slows, and we crawl along at fifteen miles an hour. The rain has stopped, but the clouds look angry, as if looking for someone to smother.

Slow and stressful, we make our way across West Virginia and into Virginia. Traffic is start and stop. Reece is frustrated and cursing. Finally, in Alexandria, we cross the Potomac River and turn off on smaller roads to reach the hotel, which takes another two hours. By the time we reach the hotel, it's one or so in the morning, and the rain is coming down like cats and dogs. Unknown to Arthur or Caroline, I have booked them into one room. Arthur is flabbergasted but relents, probably because he is so tired. Caroline seems quite happy with the arrangement.

The next morning, around eight, we're still road-lagged but head for D.C., having snacked on pretzels and sodas that I brought. What should've taken an hour and a half takes five hours. It feels like we're crawling down a long, narrow tunnel in which we can't turn around. As we approach D.C, people are hanging out of their windows, yelling and pumping their fists. Reece gets frustrated and starts taking side streets, making a dozen turns. The roadsides are packed with cars. We suddenly happen upon the Iwo Jima Memorial, and without asking, Reece pulls up over a curb onto bright-green grass.

"We're walking from here," he says like a leader should. There is a swath of people walking down the roads, further blocking traffic, and we follow along. One lady has a sign that says, "Kill Dahlia!" and I shiver.

"Such humanity," says Arthur. "We need to stay close together."

The crowd we're in is walking across the Potomac Bridge, and we muddle along, taking up an entire lane. The other lanes are completely choked. Police cars are everywhere, and there's an armored vehicle at the end of the bridge. The center of the gathering is at the National Mall, but all monuments have been closed, we learn from a police officer with a bullhorn. My main thought is, where in the world will we use the bathroom?

The crowd we have been following slows, and we have to push ahead. Arthur has become the gentleman and leads the way for Caroline, and Reece parts the mob for me. The mood is tense, and there are pockets of shouting that we can't see. We pass a man selling Julia and Dahlia hats, and we trust that we are headed the right way, focusing on the white needle of the Washington Monument to guide us. We pass more armored vehicles, many with guns and what I imagine are water cannons.

After another hour of pushing and dancing with the crowds, we arrive at the Lincoln Memorial, and it's surrounded by soldiers with rifles. Caroline is terrified but

Emma

also quite excited by the chaos. We know that something is supposed to happen at four p.m., but we're not quite sure what. We imagine there will be speeches, but are not certain where to go to hear them. I check my watch and it's three-fifteen. I'm so tired and thirsty, and lean on Reece for support. He's a darling and puts his arm around me and holds me tight as we wait for something to happen.

For an hour, we stand, crushed by what Arthur calls the humanity. We hear police and ambulance sirens in the distance. A military helicopter hovers above the Mall. The crowd is alive and buzzing, the noise deafening. We manage to get within sight of the reflecting pool, but it's like sardines in a can. Suddenly, a fat man grabs my shoulder bag from behind, and I somehow slide to the ground, fearing that I'll be trampled. I look up, and Reece has the man in a headlock. He can't get him to the ground because of the pressing crowd. I've lost sight of Caroline and Arthur, and force myself to stand. Reece has my bag and is throwing elbows at the guy, who has a bloody nose.

"Reece, stop!" I say.

`He yells at the fat man who squeezes away from his mistake. There are loud pops, and a great cry ripples through the crowd that wants to run but has nowhere to go.

"Reece!"

He grabs my arm and pulls me toward him. "You okay? Where are Arthur and Caroline?"

"Hurt my ankle," I say. "They've been swallowed by the crowd."

There's a large ruckus to our left, and the crowd bristles and sways. A woman in a halter top looks me right in the eye and says, "A Returnee! A Returnee!" She backs away from us like we have the plague. Judging by the signs, we're in a knot of Dahlia supporters. Their attention turns toward us, and Reece shields me, but someone hits me on the back of the head with a sign. Reece is shouting and posturing. A fist reaches his head, and he jerks back, then lunges at the man, losing me for a second, but I have a tight grip on his leather belt. I scream. The world has been reduced to a small vortex of chaos that we can't escape. Reece sees the need to leave and plows through the bodies like a bulldozer, pulling me along with him. A news helicopter flies overhead, adding to the noise.

Reece leads us into an area with few signs, hoping we'll be safe. It's getting so tight I can't breathe. In the distance, there is a noise that sounds like a loudspeaker, but we can't hear what is being said other than "Julia." There are distant loud pops, and a wave of panic rushes through the crush like tremors from an earthquake. Then there is an explosion that rushes up and over the Mall, followed by what must be the popping gunfire. The sky is a dirty gray, and it begins to rain. The rain is warm and weirdly refreshing in the heat. There is a press from ahead, and we are pushed back, unable to turn around.

"We gotta get out of here!" says Reece. "Watch for Arthur and Caroline!"

We move as a tight unit, shoving our way through like an icebreaker. Twenty feet ahead, a man is sitting on another man's shoulders, and he has a rifle. I scream at Reece to get down. The man begins firing, seemingly at random, and Reece leans into the masses. There is blood, and I scream again, as he crumples to the ground. People are standing on his legs and moving like disturbed hornets. The man is still firing. I'm on Reece and checking his pulse. Nothing. I die inside and scream, "Reece!" The sound of gunfire, near and far, is steady. The crowd has given us some space. I go into nurse mode and begin CPR, giving him two breaths and then compressing his chest twelve times. His eyes are blank, and I get blood in my mouth but don't care. I'm alone in the world with Reece as I continue to breathe for him and pump his chest. Sirens, gunfire, helicopters, loud explosions. It's all just background noise as I try to save his life.

My heart is dead. "Reece, Reece," I say, giving up after fifteen minutes. I'm on my knees, covered in blood and staring at his face, so young and handsome. I think about our baby and am overtaken with gasping sobs. Someone steps on my hand, and I scream for them to get away. I smooth back his mahogany hair and touch the wound just below his neck. I lick the blood from a finger as a final goodbye.

"Emma, dear God!"

I look up, and it's Arthur with Caroline behind him. His face is ashen. "Young Reece, is he with us?"

"He's with me, but he's dead," I say, and dry heave. The tears have left, and I'm getting angry. How could this happen? We should have listened to Markush and stayed home. It's partly my fault for wanting to come.

Caroline screams when she sees Reece and seems to faint, Arthur catching her. My legs have gone numb, and I can't move, as if glued to the pavement. Although soaked with blood, Reece looks so peaceful, and I can't help but think that he'll jump up and say it's all a big joke. Arthur leans over and places his hand on my shoulder. There's another explosion, and suddenly I realize that the crowd is moving over and around us. I can't believe it, but Arthur squats and manages to heft Reece onto his hip and then onto his shoulder. I can see his legs shaking and the strain on his face. Suddenly, I feel helpless and ask Arthur what to do. We must escape with Reece somehow. An ambulance is no good at this point. Amazingly, above the chaos of the throng, I see a blue dot, and the crowd gives us room. A man in a wheelchair sees our dilemma and yells for us to drape Reece across his chair. I see the logic and yell at Arthur, who nearly drops Reece onto the man's lap and then begins pushing in the general direction from which we came. It's terrible to see Reece lifeless, his limbs flopping as we meld into the horde, which has begun to move at a walking pace, although everyone wants to run. I can't specifically remember the way back to the car, but Caroline recognizes which way we should head, and I just let her lead, not knowing how keen her sense of direction is.

We pass groups of soldiers as we make it onto the bridge, which is by now filled with people, with some cars stranded amid the mob. The wheelchair man's name is Danny, and he's from Tuscaloosa, Alabama. The crowd is moving faster now, all going away from the Mall, which is clouded with smoke. Sounds of shots continue to reach us. I had forgotten that it was raining and suddenly feel very cold. It takes us nearly two hours to reach the car, which has a parking ticket on it. There's a news crew at the Iwo Jima Memorial, where we parked, and they spot us, moving in quickly for the macabre sight of Reece slung over a wheelchair. Arthur takes charge and asks them to leave us in peace. We thank Danny, and I give him a twenty, the only cash I have. I don't know what to do other than put Reece in the front passenger seat. I lean the seat back, so he won't fall forward, and we join a jumbled fray of vehicles trying to escape.

Traffic is a nightmare, cars blocking the road: ambulances, police cars, and a few Humvees. We head west on I-66, and I'm looking for the first gas station. None of us has peed since this morning. Caroline and Arthur whisper in the back seat. I can't help but glance over at Reece. His head has slid to the door window, and he looks uncomfortable, but I know he is dead. There's an exit for a gas station, and I get off into the slow line of cars. The gas station is packed, and people are milling around. I get in line for a pump that's six deep and tell Caroline and Arthur to use the restroom. Arthur leads her away with his hand on her back.

I'm alone with Reece. I adjust his head and notice that he is getting stiff. His skin is a pale yellow, his eyes partially open. His shirt is torn open, and the bloody wound below his neck looks grizzly. I want to cry, but can't, and hold his cold hand. Then it occurs to me. I fold my hands in prayer and ask Julia to save Reece. A tiny blue dot appears over the dashboard, and my heart leaps. I look at Reece, and in amazement, I watch as the color rises from his chest, into his neck, and then his face. "Reece?" The car in front moves forward, but I'm occupied with saving Reece. His fingers twitch, and his eyelids begin to move. "Reece," I say. I'm overjoyed but can't grasp that he died. A black Camaro pulls in front of me, and I blare the horn. "Reece.

Talk to me. You were shot." I notice the bullet wound has started to heal. I can see the tissue moving like in a science experiment. "Squeeze my hand." He squeezes my hand, and the blue dot disappears. A tremble passes through his body, and he opens his mouth, but no words emerge. I'm holding his hand and holding my breath that this will stick. He lifts his other hand and turns his head toward the window. He whispers.

"Reece, you're back. You were shot and died, but Julia brought you back. We're on our way..." The day crashes down on me, and I begin to shake, so afraid that I'm dreaming. Silently, I tell the baby that Daddy's okay and not to worry.

It takes a good thirty minutes to reach the pump, and Reece is coming back in bits and pieces. I think he says he loves me, but I can't be sure. "I love you, Reece. Your baby loves you." A car horn beeps behind me, and I get out and start pumping. It's evening, and the bright lights overhead make everything seem new and plastic. I have to pee like a racehorse. Finally, I see Caroline and Arthur, and they look rough from the rain, the heat, and the chaos. I motion for them to hurry up.

"There was a very long line," says Arthur. "I would—"

"He's back!" I say, forgetting about the pump. "Here, I'll open the door. Reece, look at me. It's Arthur and Caroline."

"Whatever can you mean?" asks Caroline. Both she and Arthur squint at Reece as if he were a bug.

"Have you gone mad?" asks Arthur.

"Just look," I say. "Reece, say something."

Reece's mouth moves and forms an O. "I love...you."

Emma

Caroline and Arthur lean in further, and I back away.

"Dear God, he's alive," says Arthur. "Reece, we are here to lend you aid, my young friend."

"It's a miracle," says Caroline, and she dabs at her eyes.

"Watch the pump," I say. "Reece, I have to go pee, but I'll be right back."

I rush into the store and see a line of twelve women and a line of five men. I get in the men's line because I'm about to rupture something. *Reece, alive from the dead.* Shifting from foot to foot, I wait and wait, but finally my turn comes, and I rush in, not locking the door. My drawers fall to my knees, and I'm peeing before I sit down, making a small mess. *Reece, in the car, alive and mostly well.* The car door is still open, and I put the pump back and check on Reece. He has one leg out the door as if he is about to go on a walk.

"I think he wants to stand," says Arthur. "He must be most uncomfortable."

"Reece," I say. "You want to stand up?" I reach for his hand and pull, but he's mostly dead weight.

"Home," says Reece, and I get his message.

"Come on, guys, let's go. I meant to get some honey buns but forgot." I put Reece's leg back in the car and rub his mussed hair. "We missed you, good buddy. You're back." I'm in disbelief at my own words.

Traffic is jammed, getting back onto the interstate, and it takes us over an hour to reach speeds of forty. The whole world seems to be fleeing, and Reece is alive.

MULDRAUGH

The trip home took sixteen hours, arriving on Sunday around noon. We passed several military convoys, and sonic jets streaked across the sky at times. One gas station was out of fuel in West Virginia, and there was a near-riot at the pumps. The highlight of the trip back, though, was watching Reece come alive. The longer we drove, the more he talked and moved. I explained to him what happened, and he doesn't remember being shot or dying. He said he just appeared in what he learned was Dogtown, alone. Julia magically sent him back to his body here on Earth. He had only been dead for about four hours, but he said it seemed like a million years.

We approach the Fort Knox gate to take Arthur and Caroline home, but no civilians are being allowed on base. A tank looms ominously, ready to do battle, and we do a U-turn and head home to Muldraugh. Reece says they're protecting the gold, and that makes some sense. Within ten minutes, I pull into the long driveway. Rupert is at the fence barking. That's the first thing Reece always does: pet the dog.

"Let me assist," says Arthur. Reece's walk is unsteady, and he takes Arthur's arm.

"Such a trip!" says Caroline. "We have seen the dead arise and with great cheer."

"I'm a definite believer now," I say, meaning Julia. We have all embraced Julia as the benevolent God, despite her allowing violence recently, but this act of resurrection seals the deal. "Afewerki! I was worried about you being here by your lonesome." We're in the kitchen.

"Hello! Yes, I am fine. There were many gunshots and many sirens yesterday and last night. I saw the violence in Washington on TV and have been worried about you. Reece, you are okay?"

"Yeah, but you won't believe it," says Reece. His sense of humor is back, I can tell. It's hard to keep my eyes off his face, which is very alive.

"What is not to believe?" asks Afewerki.

"I was raised from the dead!"

Afewerki frowned. "You are joking with me."

"I have to sit down first, in the living room. That drive was hell, even though I was dead for part of it." I laugh and follow him to the couch. He's walking like an old man.

"It's quite the miracle," says Caroline. She takes the overstuffed chair, and the rest of us are on the couch.

"You tell him," says Reece to me.

"There were a million people there, literally. We had to fight our way to get close to the Mall, where the monuments are. Anyway, a man with a rifle shot Reece below the neck. I did CPR, but he didn't make it. We had to escape with his body using a wheelchair."

"But he is living?" asks Afewerki.

"I asked Julia to save him, and he came back to life, and his bullet wound healed. Reece is like Jesus now," I say.

"It is the most amazing result," says Arthur, sitting with his legs crossed. I hate to say it, but he smells like he's been working in a sweatshop. We all need a shower, and I can't wait for mine."

"What a hell," says Afewerki, and I laugh. "I am not believing it, but you say it is true?"

"As true as can be," I say. "He was dead, no pulse, no nothing, for four hours. Julia brought him back."

"Well, we must thank her," he says. "I am happy that Reece is alive."

"Yeah, me too," says Reece. "I guess I've seen it all."

We all go pee, and I take a shower in the upstairs bathroom. I use Reece's sandalwood soap, and it smells so good. Washing my hair feels so good, too, and I realize I'm exhausted, having driven sixteen hours. It occurs to me we should call Markush. I'm surprised he hasn't called us. Back downstairs, Reece and Arthur are watching *CNN*. The world is falling apart, and Caroline is taking a bath.

"Estimated deaths in D.C. are around one-sixty," says Reece. "Not including me, I suppose." He laughs but stops abruptly.

"We were most lucky to escape," says Arthur.

"The Capitol is locked down. Armed forces are battling the National Guard. There's a national crisis with a curfew of nine p.m. Demonstrations and gatherings of more than ten people have been banned," says Reece. "And the list goes on."

"I'm worried about food," I say.

"Looters everywhere. Store owners are standing guard," says Reece. "Look." He points at the TV. A camera roams a drug store's aisles in Arlington, Virginia. The shelves are empty.

It's getting hard to believe, and I suggest we call Markush. Reece calls and tells the very entertaining story of our adventure in D.C. Markush is flabbergasted and tells Reece to stay put. He wants us back on base, but that's a problem at present. He says he'll work out something.

Emma

I'm curious about Reece and Alabama-Emma, so I give them a call. I feel this urgent need to talk about what happened. I'm so tired that I feel like I have rubber arms and legs.

"Reece, it's Emma."

"Which one?"

"We're still married, dummy," I say.

"You guys safe? It's chaos here. It's not safe to go out anymore. We've been holed up here, eating out of Emma's mom's freezer."

I unfold the story for him. We were caught up in a frenzy, and Reece was shot and died. Julia brought him back to life. He's seen Julia in action before and totally believes the story. He says there have been others killed and resurrected with Julia's help. I ask about Mia, and she's fine. He puts her on the phone for a minute, and we chat. She says that she likes the other Emma, but she's scared to go outside. There have been helicopters flying over their house, and she hates the sound. I hear popping noises from outside, and Rupert is barking.

"Bye, Reece. Gotta go," I say.

"Look under the bed," he says. "You may need it. I bought it before I left and forgot to bring it with me." We end the call.

Caroline emerges from the bathroom with a towel around her head. I taught her to do that. She's wearing her old black dress and sandals that I gave her. I look at her, then Reece, then Arthur, then the TV. I feel pulled in so many directions and helpless.

"Got to go to bed," I say, and I drag myself upstairs and sprawl on the bedspread. Within minutes, I'm asleep and having nightmares about being crushed in a crowd.

The next morning, around nine, I awake. Reece is beside me under the covers. I still can't believe he's alive. I hear a loud noise downstairs, and my alarm bells go off. I remember what Reece told me last night about something under the bed, and I know what it is. Underneath, I find a shiny shotgun and slide it out. It's heavy, and I go down the stairs, cradling the gun. It doesn't occur to me to wake Reece. I'm in the zone and can hear banging sounds. At the bottom of the stairs, the living room is clear, and I head for the kitchen and stop at the door. There are two strangers, teenagers, packing up our food into backpacks. I pump the shotgun and yell, "Get outta here!" At first, they freeze and then bolt for the back door, straight into Rupert, who is a big dog. I follow them outside as one goes over the fence and then the other, who loses a sleeve to Rupert. They disappear beyond the trees lining the street. I am dead calm, but suddenly panic takes over, and my legs shake.

"What the hell is going on?" It's Reece in his underwear. "There's cans all over the kitchen floor."

I can't speak, drop the shotgun, and go in for a hug. We embrace in the warm sunlight, glad to have one another.

FORT KNOX

A year later, tens of thousands have died in the quest for a true God. The Independent, Steven MacGivelry, won the election, bringing the federal government in line with Julia, but states have taken sides and follow their own leanings. The interstates are open again, and food is no longer scarce, but trouble remains.

Everyone moved back to base after the D.C. riots. Markush demanded it and threatened to take away our credit cards. We only leave for short trips to Radcliff, as there are still rogues out there with a point to prove. Afewerki is taking summer classes, but the rest of us are staying in the guest apartments. The other Reece and Emma here are fine and live next door to us. Caroline and Arthur are getting along famously. Two months ago, Markush survived an assassination attempt and only leaves base with a bodyguard. Things have finally settled down enough for old Reece and me to get a divorce, which we will do soon. He says there's a lawyer in Hueytown who will do it for $99. Organon suspended interviewing returnees, and we have much less to do. I saved this for last. I gave birth to a little girl three months ago. Her name is Iggy, which is a popular girl's name back in our universe. Reece and I are over-the-moon happy. Iggy has mahogany hair like Reece and green eyes like me. Our major regret is that our families back home will never know what happened to us, and that we have a baby.

We have two bedrooms, but it still seems tight. Iggy has a crib, but we can't resist sleeping with her at night, plus it makes breastfeeding easier.

"Reece, about ready!" I yell from the bedroom. I'm changing Iggy's poopy diaper.

"Hey, ready." He's wearing blue shorts and a Juliacon t-shirt, which is still a risky move these days. We're going for a walk with the gang around the lake.

Gradually, the group assembles in the parking lot. Caroline wears her summer dress of linen and has an umbrella for the sun. Arthur looks solid in his blue jeans and dress shirt. He doesn't like to wear short sleeves, even though it's in the nineties today. The other Reece and Emma look cute as always, wearing matching Dive Shop t-shirts. Iggy is strapped to Reece's chest, facing outward with a disgruntled look on her face. I remember, pull a floppy hat from my pocket, and put it on Iggy. She looks absolutely adorable. I get a thrill just looking at her. There's an MP jeep in the parking lot, and Arthur has a few words with the MPs.

The lake smells like mud and moss, which I kind of like. As we walk, everyone has a partner, and Arthur is leading Caroline by the elbow. Reece holds my sweaty hand, and all seems well with the world.

"How are Reece and the Emma of Alabama managing?" asks Arthur.

"They're good," I say. "Still getting married soon. March, I think."

"That's very exciting," says Caroline. "I wish them well."

"We're all invited," says Reece. "The church is supposed to be rebuilt by then." Greendale Baptist had been burned to the ground by arsonists affiliated with Dahlia. It was Emma's home church. For my Reece and me, formal religion has taken a back seat, and I'm surprised that they're doing a church wedding. Reece and I haven't been to church in over six months. We believe in Julia and call on her when needed. I would say that, overall, the country favors Julia the most.

"And when do you two lovebirds plan to marry?" asks Caroline, stepping over a limb.

I squeeze Reece's hand. "We want to get married back home, in our universe with our family present," he says.

"Yes, home awaits us all," says Arthur. "What is your plan for returning, if I may ask?"

"We're planning to travel to Ethiopia and visit the Abba Paulos," says Reece. "I'm pretty sure he can send us home, and you, too."

"Yes, that seems to be the best option," says Arthur. "I have asked Julia to send us back, but without answer thus far." He wipes sweat from his brow. It's dang hot without a cloud in the sky.

"Yeah, we've tried that too," I say. "We've talked with Markush about it, and he understands. He wants to go with us and meet the Abba again. Heck, we should all go together, but we'll need money to pay the Abba."

"Yes, he prefers coins of silver," says Arthur. "I was forced to dance at a bar for money to entice him to send me away from Gadam." He laughs at his words.

Everyone is hot and sweat stains our shirts. We perambulate, always looking left to gaze at the mossy lake. Reece and I are very serious about traveling back home via the Abba. We have tentative plans to travel to Ethiopia in a month or so on the Organon dime. It just gets more real every day. I wonder if little Iggy can make that journey, and am terrified.

After half an hour in the heat and humidity, we head toward the road and the guest house apartments. We pass around Organon, which is virtually empty except for Markush and Denise, and then walk through the parking lot.

"What shall we do now?" asks Caroline, holding Arthur's arm.

There's dead-heat silence, aside from doves cooing in the pines. My mother calls them rain crows. We have no idea what to do other than watch TV, but that gets old. Reece runs inside and brings back a Frisbee, while I change Iggy's diaper and put her in the baby recliner outside. The parking lot is empty except for my car, and we take up our spots to toss the plastic disc. Reece throws it to me, and I drop it with a grin. "Caroline!" I throw the Frisbee to her as softly as I can. The disc hits her in the chest. "It's harder than it appears to be," she says, brushing back her brown locks. "Throw it," I say. She tosses it feebly to Arthur, who stoops to catch it and goes to one knee. "Dear god!" he says. "Such a simple toy, but such an old body." We're laughing, and Arthur throws the Frisbee like a rock, and the disc wobbles and hits the ground.

"Just takes some getting used to," says Reece. He throws me a steady disc right into my hand.

"Oh, marvelous!" says Caroline. She looks happy and solid, but out of place with her long dress.

We play for another twenty minutes, and the game gets stale. It feels too much like wasting time to me, plus the heat, but I don't have any better ideas. We stand in our spots, staring at one another. Iggy starts to cry in the shade,

Emma

and Reece runs over to pick her up. He's a great dad, and I can't believe how Iggy has made us stronger, although we felt clueless in the beginning. I remember the day we brought her home. I said, "What do we do now?" and Reece said, "Well, let's read her a book," and we did.

Caroline loves Iggy and takes her from Reece. "There, my little princess, such a handsome girl." She shows Iggy to Arthur. "Say hello to your grandfather," she says.

"Dear me, how can that be, Caroline, other than wishful thinking?" asks Arthur. "I do admire the little thing, but am removed from any paternity." He pats Iggy's head like a dog's. Never having children, he's awkward with Iggy but loves to hold her.

Only two weeks to go before we head to Ethiopia for a rendezvous with the Abba Paulos. We'll fly to Rome, then to Addis Ababa, and from there, take a van to Alem Ketema, followed by a jeep to Godo. It will be me, Reece, Iggy, Caroline, Arthur, and Dr. Markush. The other Reece and Emma have decided they like it here and want to stay. Emma does not want to go back to the world where she was shot in the head. Reece and Alabama-Emma are getting married and moved up the date so that we could attend, assuming we'll be whisked away by the Abba Paulos and the Ark.

The roads are safe again, and Reece drives us in a van from the Fort Knox motor pool to the wedding in Hueytown. This is Iggy's first real adventure, and I'm nervous. She's such a good baby and loves her mommy's milk.

"I'm sure gonna miss you guys," says Markush. "I wish you could stay here, but I understand the wish to go home. I would be the same way."

"I can't wait for my mom to meet Iggy," I say.

"Are you worried that you'll end up in the wrong universe?" asks the other Reece. He's holding the other Emma's hand in his lap.

"I guess we have to trust the Abba," says my Reece.

"He's proficient," says Markush. "I'm sure he'll get you home safe and sound."

"He'd better," says the other Emma. "Got that baby to worry about."

"Yeah, I'm the most worried about Iggy," I say. "But we

have no other choice if we want to go back.

My Reece drives us straight through without a single stop, except to buy dinner at a drive-thru, and we arrive at the hotel at eight. It's still light outside when we arrive. My Reece and Markush head for the hot tub, and the rest of us settle in for the night. After half an hour, I'm anxious. Iggy is asleep, and I take her in her carrier down to the swimming-pool area and take a chair beside the hot tub where the boys are lounging. I'm not a fan of hot tubs, seeing them as a bacterial soup.

"Looking good," I say. They're sitting opposite one another with their arms resting on the tub's edge.

"Get in!" says Markush. His long gray hair is wet. He looks like he needs a cigar.

"I'll pass," I say. "Don't want to get MRSA or make Iggy sick with some traveler's fungus toes."

"Tilt Iggy up just a bit," says Reece. He sees her face and smiles.

"So many marriages and divorces," says Markush. "It's making me dizzy."

I laugh. "Well, Reece and I are waiting to get married till we get back home. That's the plan."

We chit-chat, talking about the upcoming trip to Ethiopia. We had some trouble with the visas, but Denise worked it out. We'll have thirty days as tourists, but we'll only need a few days at most, I hope. We've had our yellow fever shots, and Markush plans to take an antimalarial while we're there. After another half an hour, they call it quits, and we go back to our rooms.

The next morning, we gather for the complimentary

breakfast. The small room holds about ten tables. There's yogurt, bananas, muffins, energy bars, a pancake station, and cereal, along with coffee and orange juice, which tastes weak. I show Caroline how to peel back the lid on the yogurt, and she eats it daintily like a lady. We don't have to be at the venue until noon, and take our time. I notice two men looking our way and staring. I whisper to Reece, and he says all is well, but I'm worried some lunatic will crash our day. After eating and drinking too much coffee, we return to our rooms.

"Will we have a church wedding?" I ask Reece.

"I don't know. There's that cool, old theatre in Atlanta that we've talked about."

"I'd like to visit before we decide." I'm thinking about the wedding, but can't get our magical trip home out of my mind.

Reece sits on the bed and turns on the TV. It's *Gunsmoke,* and he goes to a news channel. There's still fighting in Wisconsin, but things have settled down overall. We're surprised when the focus shifts to a photo of Reece. The reporter announces that Reece and Emma are getting married, and the scene cuts to shots of the church from the outside.

"Holy cow," I say. "National news."

"I guess they know everything," says Reece. "I'll bet Loveless sent out a press release, which is strange to me."

We have a couple of hours before we leave, so we lie on the bed to take a snooze. I'm asleep in minutes, and Reece wakes me up. We meet the others in the lobby as Reece brings the van around. At the church, there are news vans, and we park a couple of blocks away and skirt around to a side entrance, avoiding any interviews. Inside the vestibule is cool, and we enter the sanctuary, which is lightly filled. A woman I very much recognize waves and runs over to our pew.

"Emma, I'm the bride's sister. You look just like Emma did when she was younger. This is so exciting to meet you." She reaches out, and we shake hands.

"Yeah, you look like an older version of my sister Abigail. Are there six girls and a boy in your family?"

"Yep, the same," she says. She says she has to run and look in on the bride.

"I see three of the sisters," I say, and point toward the far side of the congregation.

"Yeah, I vaguely recognize them myself."

Within twenty minutes, things get underway. The preacher takes his place in front of the communion table, looking bright and cheery. The processional begins, played by the organ and piano. We watch as Emma's mom, who looks like my mom, is escorted to the front pew. From what I know of my own dad, Emma's dad will not be welcome here.

There's a pause, and the ceremony begins. Emma enters wearing a strapless, off-white glove dress. Her boobs have been pushed up and jiggle like gelatin. Their vows are simple, and all is going well when a man stands and begins speaking. It's the dad, and he's as drunk as Cooter Brown.

"Thish not my daughter! She's the devil! God will strike...her dead!" Two men approach him and try to guide him out. I can't believe it's him and that he showed up. He gets into a shoving match with the ushers, who I vaguely recognize as friends I have back home. He falls to one knee, cursing, and two more men join the fray. They finally get him out of the sanctuary, and the wedding continues to its grand finale with Reece and Emma kissing.

In the family life center, a big gym with set tables, we gather for the reception. Markush and the other Emma and Reece, plus my Reece, take a table together. Sitting with us is the newly married Emma's sister, Sally, who is an older version of my sister Sally.

"Oh my god, I can't believe how much you look like my sister," says Sally.

"The same," I say. "I have to be honest, Sally is my favorite sister. "Where's your husband?"

"Divorced sadly. He was too much of a party animal. I miss him, though."

"And these two, spitting images of Reece and Emma," she says.

"I'm dumbfounded once again," says the other Reece. He puts his arm around Emma.

Our plates of baked chicken, rice pilaf, and green beans arrive, and the conversation dies down. There is no first dance with the dad, and we watch as Reece and Emma take the floor. They slow dance to "Nights in White Satin" by the Moody Blues. The "I love you" refrain is overwhelming, and I tear up. To end the dinner, we receive a small piece of the red velvet wedding cake with fudge icing.

After getting wine, Reece and I stand with Markush. He's been very quiet, soaking in the experience. He's wound up for the trip to Ethiopia, and the venture is weighing heavily on him.

"We'll need to bring a round of ciprofloxacin for everyone. The diarrhea there will kill you," says Markush.

"I can verify that," says my Reece with a smile.

"Yeah, me too," I say. "It's good to be prepared."

"Everyone needs to take four extra headshots for the paperwork in Addis," says Markush.

"Already done, unless I forget them," I say. A sudden rumble of thunder vibrates the building. "It's tornado weather outside."

"Better than inside," says my Reece.

After dessert, the dance floor opens with a DJ spinning eighties tunes. The first song is "I Wanna Rock" by Twisted Sister, and we get into it, working up a sweat. What's important is that we all have our own Reece and Emma.

TO ALEM KETEMA

We're on the plane! We just left Amsterdam and are headed for Rome. From there, we'll fly straight to Addis Ababa. Markush, Caroline, and Arthur are sitting together inside the 747. Reece and I are farther back. I've forgotten how stressful plane travel is, especially with a baby. She's struggling in my lap, trying to get comfortable. The huge plane has a middle aisle of seats and smells of nothing. I'm worried that Iggy will get a cold.

"Want me to hold her?" asks Reece. His face shines with an oily sheen. I can tell that he's tired like me.

"I'm good. She's settling down."

"This could be our last trip on this Earth."

"Yeah, hard to believe, but Ark travel is much quicker and less painful."

"That's what is hard to believe," he says, and I agree.

Descending into Rome, Iggy cries like bloody murder. I'm worried that her ears are not equalizing, but there's little I can do other than press her to my chest. We stay on the plane for about an hour before it takes off again, with about half the plane empty. We fly over the Mediterranean and head for Africa, wondering what will happen next. I feel bad for Markush, who will be alone if this works out with the Abba.

The airport in Addis Ababa is bustling at three in the afternoon. Our luggage is carefully screened, and we head into the fray. The air is dry and filled with the smell of burning rubber. Markush leads us toward a cab, one of those blue Lada taxis that are everywhere. It's a very tight squeeze, but we cram into the back, and Arthur takes the front seat, being the biggest. The taxi driver, a tall, skinny man with a boxed afro, asks us if we need birr, and we do. Markush gives him $500 and receives 4,000 birr, much better than the two-to-one exchange rate at the banks, although it is illegal.

Markush has done well, putting us up in the Hilton. I've been here before, in another world, and feel guilty staying in such a nice place surrounded by extreme poverty. The pool is really warm, thanks to hot water supplied by a spring. We check in, and the receptionist recognizes Arthur, and he is pleased. The halls are wide and polished, featuring a large bar with a sitting area. There's an Italian restaurant in the hotel, and we agree to meet at seven for dinner, giving us a couple of hours to relax, which Reece and I do beside the pool. The sky is cloudy and seems very close. A few others are stretched out on loungers, enjoying the warm weather.

"I've done many flips off the diving board, says Reece." He seems nostalgic.

"How can our universe be so similar to this one, although there are little differences?" I say.

"Hmm, I think that infinity is the key. There are infinite universes, and it's bound to be that there are copies."

"If you say so, soldier." Iggy squirms in my arms. We don't have a baby carrier, which is annoying. I decide Iggy is hungry, and do my best to breastfeed her, covering her with a towel. She goes to town, and I get the gushy feeling in my tummy. Reece loves my breasts, and I worry that breastfeeding will make them saggy. He laughs at that and says he can't wait till my boobs reach my knees.

At seven, we gather in the crowded restaurant and make do with a booth, which is tight. They have a child seat, thank God, and Iggy is just old enough to keep herself up. We all order pizza and beer.

"What've you guys been up to?" I say.

"Caroline and I experienced the most wonderful coffee ceremony down one of these vacuous halls," says Arthur.

"They roasted the beans and pounded them in a mortar. It was quite tasty," says Caroline. "The colorful dresses I admired, and there was a large photo of Julia."

"Coffee is a thing in Ethiopia," says Markush. "It's obligatory to serve coffee to guests, and it's often free, like here in the hotel. So, some logistics. A van will arrive at six in the morning to take us to Alem Ketema. Please be on time. It will be a six-hour journey to Alem Ketema, and then we'll take a jeep from there to Godo. Make sure you bring a bottle of water. You can buy water in the gift shop, using the birr I gave you. And use the water purification tablets, even here in the hotel. Or just drink beer."

"Shall we have breakfast before we go?" asks Caroline.

"No, we'll stop along the way and have some snacks. I'm sure there will be a big feed once we reach Godo. You know how spicy the food is, though."

"Yep, blow the top of your head off," I say.

Our handmade pizzas arrive fresh from the oven. Caroline has never had pizza before, and I laugh as she burns her mouth with a bite. We eat as if starving and order another round of St. George beer.

"Do you think an Afewerki will be there?" asks Reece. Our Afewerki has a year left for his degree, and he wants

Emma

to finish before attempting to return home.

"An Afewerki," I say. "He won't know us, though, but will remember the Reece and Emma he worked with."

"I mailed a letter to him a couple of weeks ago, saying we were coming, but no word back. Letters take weeks from here," says Markush.

The next day, which is sunny, we're up early, ready to go. The temperature dropped overnight, and it's still chilly. A Toyota HiAce van arrives twenty minutes late, and we pile in. The luggage barely fits into the back, and Arthur is holding his bag. Traffic is busy with plenty of goats on the road. To the north of the city is an escarpment that we climb toward Entoto, where there used to be an inspection station. There are no soldiers here, but there is a group of girls and women selling bread, pastries, and hot, sweetened tea. Our driver, Abrehem, stops at Markush's request, and we get our breakfast. I have a large, brown roll that is chewy, and some tea that only costs fifty cents total. A woman, laden with firewood, walks by stooped over. I feel bad for her, but there's nothing I can do to help. I see Arthur chatting up a local man who was walking by. Abrehem interprets for him.

The van is noisy, and the road rough. I struggle to hold Iggy. So far, she's been a champ, although her diaper is wet. Within a couple of hours, we pass Lemi and then take the steep, twisting road down the escarpment to the valley below. It's damn scary, and I cling to Reece's hand.

"Oh, I'm so frightened!" says Caroline.

"Such a rugged journey!" says Arthur as he bounces with the bumps.

On a particularly steep descent, we come upon a large truck that has bogged and is touching the inside wall. Abrehem uses all of the road to pull alongside and inquires, but our van is not able to pull them out, and we continue along our way. Every time, I think we've hit bottom, the road takes another dive. Finally, we reach the river valley, and the road straightens with a series of small rolling hills. We're riding with the windows up, as is the custom, and it's getting pretty hot and stuffy.

We cross a dried-up river and climb to Alem Ketema, where we will stay for the night. Hopefully, the Beselfui Hotel is still there. Reece and I spent some relaxing moments there, in another world, of course.

We're all shaken from the ride and welcome the sight of the hotel, which has a bar and restaurant, crude but efficient. The hotel is somewhat the same as I remember, a row of rooms on either side of a tin-roofed building. A large woman with a goiter greets us, speaking rapidly in Amharic. Abrehem interprets for us. The rooms are plain with a plank bed and a chamber pot. I have to pee tremendously and visit the shintabet. It's been upgraded from what I remember, but the smell of feces and urine is still strong.

It's just about one o'clock when we gather in the bar/restaurant. The owner said she has planned something special for us, and we agree to whatever that might be. The inside is dim, with light from the doorway. I can smell spice in the air, along with a vague sour note. Iggy is hot and sweaty and crying off and on. I breastfeed her to settle her down. We order a round of Johnny Walker Red, except for me, and then another. We've also requested beer, and they have St. George. I have an orange Fanta. After an hour of waiting, our food arrives on a big platter, enjera piled high with goat tibs, basically spicy cuts with no bones. It's Caroline and Arthur's first real Ethiopian food.

"Such spice, although the meat is tender," says Arthur. Beads of sweat gather on his forehead, and he looks to be in pain.

There are bottles of Ambo, the sparkling water. The enjera is soft and warm and tangy. I had forgotten how much I liked it. But the food is so spicy that I have to follow each mouthful with gulps of water. Arthur reaches to tear some enjera with his left hand, and Abrehem stops him. You can only eat with your right hand; otherwise, you contaminate the food for everyone. Arthur seems embarrassed and continues eating, but with his right hand.

"The power comes at dusk," says Markush. "Did you guys come here often? In your world?"

"Yep," says Reece. "Little vacations to relax away from the clinic."

Abrehem has a wad of enjera and meat in his fingers and holds it to my mouth. I take it as is the custom with the gursha and thank him. I take a bit of the enjera and let Iggy suck on it, but she doesn't seem to like it.

We finish, stuffed to the gills, and stare at one another. There are a few others inside, including two men playing checkers with bottle caps. A middle-aged man wearing slacks and a button-up shirt steps into the place and hesitates. He comes to our table and suddenly demands to see our passports. We learn that he is the town administrator. Everyone but Caroline has the passport with the visa. Caroline excuses herself and returns with her passport.

The man eyes each page, turning the passports to catch the best light. He coughs and places the passports on the table, and asks us where we are going. He seems satisfied and gets a beer, sitting and watching us.

"Close call," says Reece. "I wonder what type of administrator we'll find in Godo. It's about twenty years later here for us. It can't possibly be the Snake still in charge. That would suck."

"We must get you guys to the Abba. I'm worried every step of the way," says Markush. His long gray hair seems extra puffy today. "Let's meet here at eight tomorrow morning. We'll have to wait for a jeep or a truck to take us to Godo. Could take hours, and it's first-come, first-served."

I remember well how difficult it is to catch a ride and dread the details. The jeeps come to the town center, where there is a roundabout in the blazing sun. We're all a little buzzed from grease and beer, and there's nothing to do other than walk around. I suggest we walk to the site of the old Baptist Mission to see if it's still there.

We walk along a rutted dirt track that's very close to the edge of a cliff line that runs for miles. It's hot and windy. Caroline has tried to use her umbrella, but the wind is too strong, and she curses and looks to Arthur as if it's his fault. We pass a fenced weather station and then a group of boys playing soccer in a rocky field. We arrive at the old Baptist Mission compound, and there's nothing left but a gravel helipad. The fencing and buildings are gone. Abrehem says the people tore them down to build with. I show Caroline and Arthur where the warehouse and lodgings were, and they nod as if they can see them. I check my watch and it's three o'clock. We have lots of time to kill and

Emma

walk back to the other side of town, mainly passing houses made of tin sheets and little hole-in-the-wall stores. Out of boredom, I buy a pack of vanilla crème cookies for fifty cents and share with the group.

We agree to eat late, around seven, and retire to our rooms for a nap. Reece and I lie side by side with Iggy between us. I only have six diapers left and wish I'd brought more. But maybe we'll soon be home! That would rock the world.

Dinner is elaborate with different wots such as potatoes, greens, and sheep morsels in a fiery berbere sauce. Everyone drinks beer, except for Caroline, who has a grape Fanta. We eat slowly, still full from our late lunch. The place is crowded, all the tables taken. The electricity comes on, and the barmaid turns on a radio, playing Amharic music.

"Very festive," says Caroline. "But this food is much too spicy. I can barely swallow, and my scalp is sweating."

"Yep, just get another Fanta, and you'll be fine," says Markush.

The music seems to get a little louder, and a man dances by himself in a small open area. Except for me and Caroline, it's all men in the bar. Tin roof, cement floor, dim lighting, music—the bar has character. I'm holding Iggy, afraid to leave her in the room by herself. She's not so happy and tries to crawl out of my lap. Reece takes over for a while, and I eat very slowly. The dancing man has his eyes on us and shimmies our way in slow motion. He is interested in Caroline and bows to her and motions for her to dance. Caroline is confused at first, but with Arthur's blessing, she stands, and the man takes her hand.

We laugh and laugh as Caroline curtsies and doh-si-dohs, dancing as if she were a queen. She soon tires of the dance and returns to her seat, breathing quickly. The man is unhappy and tries to get her back, being a little aggressive.

"Arthur, help me," says Caroline.

"Young man, she is quite through with the dance." Abrehem interprets for us.

The man reaches and grabs Caroline's hand. She fights him off, and Arthur stands. "Away, away," he says to the man. "You are upsetting the lady."

It's tense for a moment, but the man relents and rejoins his buddy at a table with a scowl on his face.

"Thank you, Arthur, for being a gentleman," says Caroline.

"It is my pleasure," says Arthur.

It's after eight-thirty, and I'm bushed. Reece, Iggy, and I retire to our room. Our feet scuff on the cement floor. We get in bed with Iggy between us. I breastfeed her, and she falls asleep, which is excellent.

"Do you think we'll be home this time tomorrow?" I say.

"I hope so, but anything can happen. I'm mostly worried about little Iggy here," he says.

I am too, and pray to Julia for safekeeping.

GODO

We gather in the hot sun, waiting for a jeep. The road to Godo is too rough for the van, and Abrehem will wait in Alem Ketema for, hopefully, just Markush. There's no shade, and we sit on the circular wall that is the roundabout. The smell of wood smoke is heavy and pervasive. The shoeshine boys scope us out right away, and we all have our shoes shined for twenty cents each. Finally, after two hours of waiting, a rusted jeep comes, blowing its horn. Out of nowhere, a crowd of people appears, wanting a ride.

"We've got to hustle and fight our way in!" says Reece. He shoves his way to the passenger door, dragging me and Iggy behind him. I crawl in and take the prime seat. Arthur and Caroline manage to squeeze into the back seat with two others, and three have crammed into the very back. "We'll ride on top!" says Reece, and he and Markush climb aboard for what will be a jolting ride.

The jeep turns around and chugs out of the village, jerking with each gear shift. There's a long descent to a river valley, and then we cross two fairly dried-up rivers on Bailey bridges. The ascent to Godo is steep and twisting, just like I remember it. We pass farmers with plows and children with goats, all of humanity at work in this remote region. I hope Reece and Markush have not fallen off. After nearly two hours, which seemed like ten, I can see the village up ahead, huts enclosed within living fences. We disembark in a hurry, the driver ready for his next trip back to Alem Ketema.

Where the clinic used to be is just a vacant lot. The fence is gone, along with the clinic and the grain warehouse. A group of children has spotted us and stares with grins. "Ferenj!" says one, and then the other. We don't have an interpreter any longer, so we must find Afewerki first. Reece and I know the way to his house, assuming it's the same in our universe, and we locate his family's compound, fenced in with poles and living desert plants.

"Hallo!" yells Reece. Smoke ekes out of the main hut. Afewerki's house is a few feet away but has a tin roof.

A woman emerges with an alarmed look. It's his mother, and I step through the fence. She looks like a ghost and babbles in Amharic.

"Afewerki?" I say, asking about her son.

"Afewerki, yellum."

I step toward her, and she takes a step back. I imagine that our age stymies her. She knew the other Reece and Emma many years ago, and now it looks as if we have not aged. The people are superstitious and wary of evil spirits. I wonder how Julia has affected this place. The poverty is still evident, but at least no one appears to be starving.

A young man enters the compound, and it's Afewerki's oldest brother, Tefari, and he speaks English. I explain to him that we are looking for Afewerki, but he tells us that he has moved to Addis Ababa to work for the Ministry of Agriculture. I hate we will not get to see him, and we ask Tefari if he will take us to the Abba Paulos. He's puzzled by our presence and our ages and seems afraid of Arthur. He agrees, but first, his mother wants to do a coffee ceremony for us. It's around two, and we could use some coffee, but I know it will take forever.

Emma

We sit inside the main hut, with a fire burning and the smoke rising up the middle to filter through the straw roof. The room smells dusty and musky. The floor has recently been smoothed with cow manure, and that adds to the aroma. Abebe, Afewerki's mother, sets about the ceremony, roasting beans on a square of metal over a charcoal burner. Silent, she pushes the beans around with a short stick as if time does not exist. She crushes the beans coarsely and pours the grounds into a clay pot that sits in a basket base. Boiling water completes the process, but we wait for another ten minutes as the coffee brews. Tefari is very curious about us and asks a thousand questions. Without getting too supernatural, we explain to him that we are here to see if the Abba Paulos can send Reece and me home. He appears confused and alarmed as he shares our story with Abebe.

Afewerki's father arrives, having heard the news, holding a long knife that looks bloody. All he can do is grin and stare at us, which is uncomfortable. He says he's grateful for Reece bringing Afewerki to the States for college, and we reiterate that's another Reece.

Markush is keen that we see the Abba as soon as possible, and we head out to find him, led by Tefari. It's the same as I remember, as we pass an Orthodox Church, and soon reach where the shelter used to be for mothers and kids. The path narrows and descends, following a ridgeline to our right. Tefari stops us and points up the ten-foot wall of rock. He quickly climbs, but Caroline is reluctant, and Arthur has to coach her up. She gets maybe a foot up and falls back.

"Whoa, my dear," says Arthur. He catches her.

"I cannot climb this steep rock," says Caroline. "It will be the death of me."

Tefari has been watching and puts down a crude ladder, which is barely long enough. After some swearing, we're all at the top, and I listen for the sound of the Abba's pick on rock, but all is silent. The Abba's small hut is to our right, and we walk that way. Tefari is first to the door and calls out for the Abba, but there is no reply. He jogs over to the green door in the rock face and peers inside, then enters. Within thirty seconds, he's back outside.

"There is bad news," says Tefari. "The Abba has died."

"Oh no!" I say.

"The poor man," says Arthur.

Reece enters the church in the rock, and I follow. The Abba lies on his side, on top of his pick. There's no pulse. He died doing his life's work of carving a church from the rock. We're at a loss for what to do next. Have we traveled eight thousand miles for nothing?

"Jeez, what do we do now?" asks Reece. We're all very hot but not sweating in the arid air.

"Caroline," says Arthur, "you have some experience with operating the Ark before us. You were naughty and wore the Abba's jeweled vest out of curiosity."

"Yes, I am quite capable with this seeming magic." Caroline looks like a nineteenth-century doll in her long linen dress. "We must retrieve the vest."

"We should carry the Abba to his bed," says Tefari.

Arthur and Reece help him get the thin Abba over his shoulder, and Tefari lays down the cold body, which has begun to stiffen. The Abba looks peaceful lying there, but

I put a piece of cloth over his face. There's a small trunk beside the bed, and Caroline opens it as if it were hers. Inside is the holy raiment studded with precious stones that the Abba wears when communing with Dahlia. We assume it will work with Julia as well.

Caroline takes on an important air and leads us back to the rock chamber. It's about two hundred feet square with three pillars that have been left in place. The rock is hard and gray, and the room smells of dust. Caroline positions herself behind the bier, where the Ark will rest, if it comes.

"Okay, guys," says Markush. "Good luck."

We all say our goodbyes, as if this is going to work. Markush exits and closes the green door, sending us into darkness.

"You can do this," says Reece.

"Careful, my boy. There must be an equilibrium of spirit. Everyone kneel," she says.

We kneel in front of a wooden platform, and I close my eyes, hugging Iggy to my chest. Reece is beside me with his hand on my back.

"Julia, hear me now, dear Julia. We are but your servants. Pray, come and send us back to our homes that are so far away." I peek, and she is holding her arms in the air with a determined look.

There is a roar, and a great light that flashes blue. I can see the light with my eyes closed.

"It's here! It's here!" shouts Caroline. "I have called the Ark!"

My eyes open, and I see the golden Ark with the two cherubim on top, facing one another with wings spread. There's static playing between the wings.

"And now, we ask in all humility, send us home!"

There's more static, then a glowing ball turns into the face of Julia. She does not speak and fades as the light from the Ark grows bright and blue. There's a crash and something like a giant vacuum cleaner.

PELL CITY, ALABAMA

I groan and spit out bits of grass. Reece is on his back, stunned. I look around, wondering where we are. Then it hits me.

"Reece! Reece! Iggy's gone!" I stand and wobble, watching Reece slowly come around. I go back to my knees. "Reece!"

"Iggy, we have to find her," he says with difficulty. "We're in Pell City. This is my grandparents' house."

We split up and scour the yard that surrounds the house. I peer into shrubs and scan the front porch. A woman comes to the door and opens it. "Is this your baby?" she says. "Did you put it in our house?"

"Reece!" I yell, then rush up to who I assume is Reece's grandmother and take Iggy from her. "Oh, Iggy, little Iggy." She looks at me and smiles, then begins rooting, and I sit on the porch swing to nurse her.

"Holy cow!" says Reece. "Granny! Iggy!" He doesn't know which way to turn.

"Reece! Where have you been? You've been missing for months, boy," says Granny. Reece runs onto the porch and gives her a big hug.

"I'm back, thank God," he says.

"Horace, come quick!" says Granny, whose name is Dora.

Reece runs into the house, and soon he reappears with Horace. "Meet my family," he says, pointing at me. "This is Emma, and we're married. That's our baby girl, Iggy."

"Iggy is such a pretty name," says Dora. "And how in

the dickens are you married?"

As we talk, we move into the cool and dim living room. The house is old with high ceilings and cracked plaster here and there. The pink carpet feels like it's three inches thick. I sit with Iggy on the loveseat, and Reece joins me. Dora and Horace take recliners.

"I just looked in the guest bedroom, and there was a baby in the middle of the bed. I thought, Lord, Lord, what is going on?" asks Dora.

"A real shocker," says Horace. "And this is your baby? And your wife? How did that happen?"

Over the next hour or so, we tell them the story of Dahlia and how we were transported to another world. They take it surprisingly well. I'm so happy that we were able to make it back, and I want to get to Atlanta pronto to see my family, especially my mother. Reece and I are worried about Arthur and Caroline, hoping they made it safely as well.

So, we are home, which is so sweet. It looks like for every Reece, there has been an Emma. Reece and I bonded, working in the clinic together, and fell in love. We've had to travel the universes to be together finally, and it was all worth it. Julia is definitely in control, and I look forward to a more peaceful world. I glance at Iggy and then at Reece. I guess it was just meant to be.

THE VOX HUMANA SERIES BY RUSSELL HELMS

Famine
Struggle Me This
Half Smile
Finding Her
The Icelanders
Anywhere and Everywhere
Mother Time
Emma